ONE HEART AT A TIME

also by J. RONALD KNOTT

AN ENCOURAGING WORD
RENEWED HEARTS, RENEWED CHURCH
The Crossroads Publishing Co.   1995

ONE HEART AT A TIME

Renewing the Church in the New Millennium

J. RONALD KNOTT

with Becky Jo Hollingsworth

SOPHRONISMOS PRESS   LOUISVILLE, KENTUCKY

ONE HEART AT A TIME
Renewing the Church in the New Millennium

Cover Design: J. Ronald Knott
Book Layout & Design: Becky Jo Hollingsworth

First Printing: March 1999
ISBN: 0-9668969-0-4 (pbk)
Library of Congress Catalog Card Number: 99-94071

Printed in the United States of America

MORRIS PUBLISHING
3212 East Highway 30 • Kearney, NE 68847 • 1-800-650-7888

To

CHRISTY BROWN

who put a foundation under my dream

ACKNOWLEDGMENTS

My first collection of homilies, *An Encouraging Word*, was published in 1995 by Crossroads Press in New York. After that book underwent a second printing, it was my dream to tell, as Paul Harvey would put it, "the rest of the story." That first book dealt with the concept of God's "unconditional love." This second collection of homilies answers the question that so many people asked me after reading *An Encouraging Word*: "Where does one go after one grasps the fact that God loves us without condition?" The answer is simply this: after conversion comes transformation.

In the first book, I spoke of "conversion" as waking up to the fact that we are loved by God, without condition. In this second book, I speak of "transformation" as that gradual change which is possible within us once we have been awakened to and cooperate with God's unconditional love. This second collection of homilies is dedicated to all those who first heard, or later read, my first collection of homilies and asked, "Where do I go from here?"

I decided to "self publish" this collection of homilies instead of editing it for national publication as I did with *An Encouraging Word*. In choosing to keep the text specific and not generic, I realize that broader audiences may not recognize some local details and references. But this book is, in reality, one last gift to the parishioners of the Cathedral of the Assumption. For that reason, I want them to have these homilies and talks in a form close to the way they originally heard them.

There is no way to remember and name everyone who has influenced me as I wrote these homilies over the years, but I must acknowledge two books in particular that accidentally fell into my lap many years ago and have influenced me deeply — As You Think by James Allen and The Aquarian Conspiracy: Personal and Social Transformation in the 1980s by Marilyn Ferguson. Neither would be called "religious" books, but both are "spiritual" at their base. Along with these authors and others whose words echo in the homilies that follow, I thank the hundreds and hundreds of people who took the time to write me after hearing these homilies in their original setting through the years. Their notes and letters fill several large boxes. Their input both nourished and directed me.

It takes a host of people bring a book to print. To Archbishop Thomas C. Kelly, OP, who entrusted the Cathedral pulpit to me from 1983 to 1997; to the Cathedral of the Assumption parish council; to the Cathedral staff, especially Father Martin Linebach who so ably shared the preaching and pastoral responsibility with me in my last years there. To Christy Brown (President) and Trish Pugh Jones (former Executive Director) with whom I shared leadership of the Cathedral Heritage Foundation, I offer my deepest gratitude. A very special thanks goes to the hundreds of faith-filled lay ministers who evolved from within the parish during those intense years. It was from this community of believers that I received the consistent inspiration and encouragement I needed to preach week in and week out.

I wish to thank those who are carrying on the ministry that I was so fortunate to be part of while I was pastor of the Cathedral of the Assumption: Rev. William Fichteman, the current pastor; Rev. Martin Linebach his associate; Mrs. Pat Sexton, Director of the Cathedral Parish School of Catholic Spiritual Growth and Education and Sister Marylee King, SCN, the main spiritual teacher in that school. A very special thanks to Becky Jo Hollingsworth, former chairperson of the Cathedral Formation Committee and editor of both collections of homilies. Without her valuable work and consistent encouragement, neither book could have been brought to print. I am especially indebted to her for collecting, organizing and putting into writing the valuable feedback found in the final chapter of this book.

Finally, I thank the scores of good people who are presently enrolled as spiritual seekers and who carry on the ministries of spiritual nourishment in the Cathedral Parish School of Spiritual Growth and Education.

Contents

——— ♥ ———

A Support System for a
Community of Changing Hearts
A Parish School of Spiritual Growth and Education

I have done my share of institutional criticism. . . . But what offends me is the romantic notion that all the ills of the church reside within the institution — so that if only we could reform it, we ourselves would be better Christians. The truth quite often is the other way around.

Kenneth Woodward
Commonweal
September 8, 1994

Introduction

*...that I might know how to speak to the weary a
word that will rouse them.*

ISAIAH 50:4

——— ❤ ———

What does one say to a congregation in need of revival? What does one say to disheartened Catholics in need of renewal? I pondered these questions on a daily basis from 1983 to 1997. Living out the answers to these questions became the primary focus of my life when Archbishop Thomas C. Kelly called me from a thriving rural parish to the heart of the city to "do something with the Cathedral." The one hundred and forty-year old cathedral church of the archdiocese of Louisville, Kentucky was typical of crumbling, monumental, center-city churches in many communities. It was being given artificial respiration by a handful of dedicated (mostly elderly) parishioners. The total membership of the Cathedral of the Assumption was one hundred and ten people. It felt more like a dusty museum than a fountain of spiritual energy.

Not long after I moved to Louisville, the Archdiocesan Director of Planning suggested to me that it might be a good idea to just go ahead and close down the old Cathedral, then designate one of the newer, busy suburban parishes in Louisville as our "cathedral." He did not realize it, but as far as I was concerned, he had just thrown down the gauntlet. I took this as a challenge and sharpened my focus even more on the urgent need to discover the answers: What does one say?

Fourteen years later, the Cathedral of the Assumption

had become one of the largest parishes in the diocese and one of the most energetic parishes in the country. The Cathedral serves its over two thousand members through an array of ambitious programs. The Cathedral has become an interfaith spirituality center for the whole community through its unique partnership with the Cathedral Heritage Foundation.

In June, 1997 I ended my fourteenth years as pastor leading the renewal of the Cathedral of the Assumption Parish through the transformation of its individual members. I feel the need to write about what happened there, how a dying parish became a large, vibrant community of changed hearts, often by intuition as much as by intention. What has worked there may work, with appropriate adaptation, in other places.

What follows is a collection of homilies, talks and reflections preached at the Cathedral of the Assumption during a decade of rapid growth. It is a record of group spiritual direction by a pastor from a pulpit. These talks and reflections are invitations to spiritually hungry people to become "new creations." These homilies challenge a group of people to choose deliberate spiritual growth rather than settling for a religion that is comfortable, static, safe — but lifeless. These homilies invite those with ears to hear to become intentional Christians and conscious Catholics by choosing to walk a path of deliberate spiritual growth. They are invitations to individual discouraged Catholics to become a "new you" in a community of changed hearts.

This book is not one of those "how to" books about setting goals and objectives, drawing organizational charts or creating healthy group dynamics in your congregation. It is about presenting the idea of personal transformation as a method of revitalizing a parish. It is my belief that many,

many people must be taught that every individual must become willing to be renewed spiritually if they truly desire a renewed parish. This process rests on the belief that no church can be strong when every member of it is weak. Strengthened individuals strengthen the church.

This book is about teaching ready and willing Catholics how to be their own spiritual directors, if need be, by taking charge of their own spiritual growth. There are enough spiritually hungry Catholics out there to fill most of the empty parishes in this country! In urging individual parishioners to assume responsibility for continuing to mature spiritually I do not mean to suggest that there is no need for spiritual teachers. In our society, the idea of a spiritual teacher, instructor or religious authority is conspicuous by its absence, perhaps because such authorities have so often demanded conformity instead of leading the spiritual seeker to explore the inner path as unique individuals. As Thomas Merton commented in *New Seeds of Contemplation*:

> No one can become a saint or a contemplative merely by abandoning himself unintelligently to an oversimplified concept of obedience. Both in the subject and in the one commanding him, obedience presupposes a large element of prudence and prudence means responsibility. Obedience is not the abdication of freedom but its *prudent use* under certain well-defined conditions.

I am a product of the seminary system of the sixties. Before I came to believe in the principle of "church transformation through individual personal transformation," I had to lay aside a long-valued, older principle that was popular during my study for the priesthood and for most of the time

3

I have been a priest. I had to give up the romantic notion that church transformation is guaranteed by making structural and organizational changes in the world-wide institution or the local parish. In my twenty-eight years in ministry, I have witnessed many structural and organizational changes that have had little real impact. I have become convinced that transformation does not happen by making changes in the world outside us. Instead, with God, we co-create this miracle from within, one grateful heart at a time. Changed hearts then change the church. It's about each person changing, not making changes.

I have also had to lay aside another long-cherished, but mistaken belief popular throughout the years I have been a priest. I have watched attempts to replace religious symbols with social service, political action and psychotherapy. While I am proud of the development of social teaching in the Catholic Church in this century and appreciate the fact that social commitment is essential in Catholic Christianity, social and political commitments are a consequence of, not a substitute for, religious faith. If Mother Teresa of Calcutta has taught us anything, it is this — social action by the Church must be rooted in the gospel, grounded in a balance between action and contemplation, or it is just social work.

All this may strike some as sounding "new age." It isn't. Though organized religion has produced several articles and books scornful of this "new age movement," this trend has made a valuable contribution. The sterility of organized religion gave birth to this movement, revealing a rapacious appetite for spiritual growth that organized religion is failing to feed. The biggest weakness of this movement is its tendency to focus on "individualism" to a degree that borders on narcissistic. In *New Seeds of Contemplation*, Thomas Merton speaks of the peril of the spiritual seeker who ignores the essential balance provided by a spiritual teacher within a community.

> The most dangerous man in the world is the contemplative who is guided by nobody. He trusts his own visions. He obeys the attractions of an interior voice, but will not listen to other men. He identifies the will of God with anything that makes him feel, within his own heart, a big, warm, sweet interior glow. The sweeter and the warmer the feeling, the more he is convinced of his own infallibility. And if the sheer force of his own self-confidence communicates itself to other people and gives them the impression that he is really a saint, such a man can wreck a whole city or a religious order or even a nation. The world is covered with scars that have been left in its flesh by visionaries like these.

The privatization of the gospel, indeed any excessively individualistic interpretation of the Christian message, is a distortion of the Christian religion. Jesus preached conversion and the coming of God's kingdom. Jesus taught that the good news of God's unconditional love had social, as well as personal, meaning. Organized religion has come a long way in its social teaching, but in the process, it has neglected its mystical tradition and the personal dimension. This book is about personal spiritual transformation <u>within</u> the community of the church. This book is about a personal transformation that infuses all parts of a person's life. Religion needs personal transformation to give it soul and the experience of personal conversion needs religion to give it depth and breadth.

Transformation follows conversion. Conversion is God's action in opening one's eyes to life in God's unconditional love. Transformation is about engagement with life itself, as a grateful response to God's love. Bernard Lonergan discusses conversion in these terms as well. In his 1972 book *Method in Theology* he says:

> Operative grace is the replacement of the heart of stone by a heart of flesh, a replacement beyond the horizon of the heart of stone. Cooperative grace is the heart of flesh becoming effective in good works through human freedom. Operative grace is religious conversion. Cooperative grace is the effectiveness of conversion, the gradual movement towards a full and complete transformation of the whole of one's living and feeling, one's thought, words, deeds, and omissions.

My first book, *An Encouraging Word,* was about the conversion experience of realizing that God loves you unconditionally. Transformation is that ongoing process of growth, rooted in the soil of self-esteem that flows from accepting God's unconditional love. Transformation requires a conscious decision to respond to God's generous love through disciplined attention to the inner path Christ taught. This book is about conscious self-growth, discipleship if you will; about what you do after you wake up. It's about committing oneself to the inner work that will manifest itself in all aspects of one's life: community, church, parish, workplace, family and marriage.

In this fourteen-year process, I have learned five important things. (1) In a culture disappointed with materialism, people are hungry for spiritual growth, even disaffected Catholics both inside and outside the church. Feed them and they will come. Converted hearts need somewhere to go. Many more people hunger for spiritual growth than there are places in the church that will feed them. Seeking alternatives to their unsatisfactory experiences in parishes and disenchanted with the look of spirituality they find there, people are crossing religious lines, denominational lines and even state lines to find spiritual nourishment. (2) Individuals approach, experience and practice both the exoteric and the esoteric aspects of religion. The exoteric aspect is concerned with the forms of religion, with correct adherence to the rituals, officially approved practices, and precepts of a particular faith or wisdom tradition. Those who follow this exoteric approach to religion are content to relate only from a distance with the transcendent. The focus of the esoteric approach, a contemplative tradition which might guide them to a more intimate relationship with "ground of their being," is concerned with the essence of religion. Recent Catholicism has, I believe, become much too exoteric in its focus. We have lost contact with our own spiritual growth tradition. (3) By learning to distinguish the medium from the message, even inactive Catholics, some of whom have been hurt deeply in the past, can be led to freely choose their Catholicism and can learn to view the institution with adult compassion. (4) Transformation cannot be taught; it must be described, modeled, experienced, lived and shared through stories. People can be pointed toward transformation, given the opportunities to experience it, and provided with the tools they will need to foster the process. (5) Transforming people ask for religious education, reformation of the structures and opportunities for service. The institution in which they transform is transformed in the process. When enough people commit to work with God toward their own transformation, there will be no need to resort to overly detailed legislation and authoritarian intimidation as a way to maintain the church.

How does one revive a dying parish? It's simple. All you have to do is lead the ones who will spearhead the revitalization to consciously commit to their own serious spiritual transformation, then encourage them to talk about it with passion, regularity, clarity and conviction. Since people are already spiritually starving and looking for spiritual energy, they will hear about it. Little by little, those people who are ready for spiritual transformation will find these teachers. When enough of these seekers and teachers gather together and begin to intersect and interact, they will wake up one day and realize that the parish has been revitalized!

In the new millennium, let's seek to renew the church not by manipulating structures, but through graced personal conversion and courageous transformation, one heart at a time.

A Change of Heart:
The Exciting Possibility of a
New You

— ♥ —

Not Conform, Inform or Reform, But Transform

Do not conform yourselves . . . but be transformed by the renewal of your mind.

ROMANS 12

———— ❤ ————

My life can be divided into two parts: 1944 to 1966, and 1966 to the present. Using St. Paul's terms, the operative word in the first part was "conform." The operative word for the second part is "transform."

Until I was about twenty-two years old, I lived my life by taking cues about my direction from the world around me. I was told from the very beginning of my life that I would be valuable and acceptable if I would simply do as I was told. "We wouldn't be having all these problems if you would simply do as I tell you" seemed to be one of my Dad's favorite lines. I tried my best to conform as a way of getting his approval. Most of my efforts failed, usually triggering another of his favorite lines: "You can't do anything right." So, no matter how hard I tried to conform, tried to figure out how to please him and how to get his approval, I failed. All my attention was on him; trying to predict what he wanted, trying to figure out how to please him, and trying to prevent the constant rage that inflicted our home.

I quickly learned I could never be good enough, could never do anything "right" so I developed another technique for survival — become invisible. I began to believe that if I would simply stay out of sight, I could prevent at least a few of the painful encounters. In all this, it was easy for me to believe I was indeed defective. All my attention and energy went toward trying to figure out how to survive in an insane world. I was much older before I understood that my father had some serious problems which had nothing to do with me. I understand now. I harbor no resentment. In fact, my compassion for him grows as the years go by.

When I left my family home to attend the seminary in 1958 at the age of thirteen, I definitely entered another world of conformity. As I had learned to do at home, I concentrated all my attention and energy on trying to understand and please some very demanding adults. The theory of seminary education in those years was to "break us" of any individuality and to "mold us" into obedient servants of the church. The minor seminary used a "military school" model.

No matter how hard I tried, I could not seem to conform to what often appeared to me unreasonable, certainly unpredictable, wishes. I was almost "discharged" in my sophomore year of high school seminary. The rector referred to me, to my face, as a "hopeless case." By the grace of God, I was given one last chance to "shape up." Through all this, I usually relied on my childhood coping skills. I became an expert at becoming invisible. It was blend in, avoid risks, make no waves and have no opinions. I had no idea who I was in those days. Still, I survived for six years and I graduated.

In 1964, I entered St. Meinrad Major Seminary. I did not realize it at the time, but I had just entered another, very different world. In the words of St. Paul, I had left the world of "conform" and entered the world of "transform." Instead of taking cues from **outside** myself as I had always done, I was about to make a radical shift and begin to take cues from **inside** myself.

Instead of trying to force fit us into some predetermined mold, these Benedictine monks were talking about individuality, personal gifts and talents, developing our uniqueness. It was Chinese to me! I had always been taught that I was defective, a condition with a poor prognosis for repair. At St. Meinrad, my teachers talked about helping me identify my gifts and talents. Even more astonishing to me, they said they expected to help me develop these alleged talents, making them bloom.

Instead of feeling relieved, I became even more terrified. I thought to myself, "My God, what am I going to do when these people start digging around inside me and find out there isn't anything there?" I had no sense of myself as one who had either gifts or talents. I employed my trusty old coping mechanism in an effort to postpone discovery by my new teachers. I became invisible. By this time, I was very clever at this game. I was neither to be seen nor heard.

It was during my second year at St. Meinrad that I had a major conversion experience. It occurred on a fire escape between classes. Like a bolt of lightning, in what had to be a great moment of grace, I somehow made the decision to cooperate with God in saving my own life. I decided to become a self. I decided that I was going to "live happily ever after," and I could not leave it up to others. I decided to act boldly on my own behalf. I decided to "get a life," to become the co-creator of my own life, and quit being a victim. I decided to take my cues from "in here" rather than "out there" and to be passionate about it. This was no half-hearted pledge to go on some kind of diet or exercise program. It was a complete and total change of mind, heart and spirit. It came from the center of my being. It came

13

from God.

This, I believe, is what St. Paul is talking about when he says "be transformed by the renewal of your mind" rather than "conform yourselves to this age." Paul himself had spent most of his life "conforming" to an elaborate religion of external observances. He was a Pharisee. Pharisees were people who slavishly and meticulously conformed to the most minute rules and rituals of organized religion. He was good at it, but never good enough, he thought. No matter how perfectly he observed the rules, St. Paul never felt good enough for God. Then one day, in a blinding flash of insight, it hit him! He made a 180° turn in his thinking, a complete and total regeneration of mind, heart and spirit. He learned what conversion is all about. Conversion is **not** about doing things to get God to love us. It **is** about waking up to the fact that God has loved us all along. It's not about external conformity, but the beginning of becoming a new creation! It's about building ourselves from the inside out! Yes, it **really is** about being "born again."

One of the defects of our culture is our obsession with being conformists. Why else would some of our kids kill each other over a pair of Reeboks? We would rather mimic the lives of others than create our own. We would rather watch sports than play them. Soap operas, romance novels and pornography replace real intimacy for millions of lonely people. We dress like clones, build houses like clones, and pick our cars like clones. We still peck non-conformists to death, one way or another! We would still rather put our heroes on pedestals than try to become heroic ourselves. We want certain people to be religious **for** us and we crucify them when they aren't, because it's a whole lot easier than being religious ourselves. We would rather conform than transform. We would rather "make changes," than

14

"change." We would rather mimic someone else's life than get a life.

One of the defects of my religious upbringing was the assumption that religion is primarily about informing, conforming and reforming; assenting to certain facts, following certain rules and correcting certain behaviors. As important as all these are, they are not of the essence. This is why many lay people and religious still think the problems of the church could be solved if people at the top would just "make some changes," while highly placed clerics still believe that the solution lies in obedience from the people at the bottom. What is **really** needed in our church, from top to bottom, is not more "changes," but more "changing," that complete and total regeneration of mind, heart and spirit through which individuals experience a rebirth. This "changing" begins with conversion of thinking and leads to individual personal transformation. If enough of us did that, the necessary "changes" would become obvious and acceptable to everybody involved.

"Transformation" must be preceded by a conversion of thinking. "Transformation" requires a conscious decision to go on a spiritual journey that sparks an interior revolution. "Transformation" follows the choice to look inside rather than looking outward. "Transformation" flows from a decision to change our minds about who we are and then, with God's help and at God's instigation, a commitment to begin acting boldly on our own behalf. An openness to the process is the beginning and is often followed by a "conversion experience" that leads to a radical change in one's person, nature, disposition and heart. For me it happened on a fire-escape. For St. Paul it happened on the road to Damascus. For everybody who has had one of these experiences, it is a moment of grace — sudden, unpredictable and wonderfully

15

energizing, but certainly not magic. The adventure having begun, the inner work still has to be done.

St. Paul summed up the spiritual life this way: "All that matters is that we become new creatures." When we understand that, and when we accept the task of becoming our own spiritual directors, we have understood the difference between "conform" and "transform," the difference between religion and spirituality. Yes, we will have understood who we are and what to do about it!

August 29, 1993

On Becoming Somebody New

All that matters is that one is created anew.
Galatians 6

——— ♥ ———

Talk shows, as a general rule, make me sick. Some of our planet's most pathetic people are put on exhibit like freaks in a cheap circus, and prodded into spilling their guts for the whole world to pick through. But I have to confess to you that one day recently I was channel-surfing, and before I knew it I was seduced into watching one of those talk shows.

They were doing "make-overs" on this particular show. The host ushered out several very ordinary looking men and women and put them on exhibit. Then these people were whisked away to be "made-over" by hair stylists and fashion experts. At the end of the show the guests paraded back on stage to the "oohs" and "aahs" of the cheering crowd. A pot-bellied, rough-looking man came out wearing a silk suit and sporting blow-dried hair. A greasy-haired teenager in a sweatshirt reappeared with a bouncy hairdo, modeling a tailored suit. The premise of this show was that you can indeed become a "new person" simply by investing in new "hairdos" and "duds." This is certainly not the "new creation" about which St. Paul speaks in our second reading.

Several years ago I read that all the cells in the human body are replaced with new ones once every seven years. In other words, we get a totally new body about every seven years. According to those calculations, I am now into my eighth body. As I look it over, I must admit that this too is not the "new creation" of which St. Paul speaks in the letter to the Galatians.

> *It doesn't matter whether one has been circumcised or not. All that matters is that one is created anew.*

In this passage, Paul is talking to a bunch of people who had undergone circumcision, as if that external physical "make-over" made them "religious," impressed God, and made them "holy." It was a little like some of us getting crosses tattooed on our arms, thinking that would make us "Christian." Some didn't even undergo circumcision for religious reasons, but because they wanted to save their rear ends in case of persecution. If they were circumcised, they would be left alone by Jews and Romans alike. It would be like getting yourself baptized so you could have a certificate to gain admission to a private school. Paul says that none of these external religious gymnastics make one bit of difference! What does make a difference is what happens **inside** of you, not outside of you. All that matters is that we are in the process of becoming new people.

My friends, there are two paths you can take in this life, two worlds that you can explore. One path promises happiness through the accumulation and rearrangement of material reality — a new hairdo, new "duds," a bigger house, a better job, another spouse, more recognition. The other path, the one that only a few discover and explore, is an inner spiritual path which promises happiness through personal discipline — a conscious dedication to the truth, an ability to stand up to one's own addictions, a genuine and heartfelt love for oneself, a deep compassion for every other human being. This is an inner struggle.

Christian spirituality is the discipline of becoming an

increasingly happy and whole person as a baptized child of God. This, I believe, is what Paul means by "becoming a new creation." "Becoming a new creation" is about answering God's call to be all that we can be!

"Becoming a new creation" begins with imagining yourself as the shaper of your own life with the help of God. Like an artist, you add and subtract, creating a new and better person over and over again. If you can imagine it, you can do it. You "do it" by taking charge and taking responsibility for the life God entrusted to you. You can not think yourself into a new person; you must act your way into being a new person. This discipline can be learned. You start with some small things and, through dedication to the path, you soon learn that you can take on bigger and bigger issues. There will be setbacks. But each time you overcome a setback, you realize that you have become stronger in the process. Spirituality is about this "pursuit of happiness." Spirituality is about being intentional in doing hard things for your own good. The ability to carry through on those intentions makes it possible for one to become a new creation, a new self.

Once you discover the spiritual world of intentional living, you will begin to discover that religion can offer the spiritually-evolving person structures and disciplines for growth. Religion supplies the tools. Religion is not God. It points to God.

There is one warning about setting out to become a new person. You must first give up thinking of yourself as a mistake who needs to be fixed before you are OK. You must learn to see yourself as basically good, with limitless possibility for growth and depth. It's really a matter of caring enough about ourselves to be good to ourselves. Again, not in a self-indulgent way, but caring enough about ourselves

19

to do difficult things for our own good. "Becoming a new person" is hard work. It takes self-discipline and patience. It is not for cowards and the lazy.

Let me close by sharing this quote from an unknown writer which came across my desk last week: "You have immense potential to love, to care, to create, to grow, to sacrifice, if you believe in yourself. It doesn't matter your age, or your color, or whether your parents loved you or not. Let that go, it belongs to the past; you belong to the now. It doesn't matter what you've been, the wrong you've done, the mistakes you made, the people you've hurt. You are forgiven. You are accepted. You're OK. Give yourself a new birth. Begin now. Today."

"All that matters is that one is created anew."

July 9, 1995

The Second Call

———— ♥ ————

There is a world of difference between being a disciple and being one who dabbles in religion. A disciple is a serious student who freely attaches himself or herself to a religious teacher intending to learn to live life as taught by that teacher. The disciple wants to emulate, not just imitate. In contrast, the dabbler in religion may know a few religious facts, may wear religious jewelry, may attend religious functions and even be on the roster of some religious sect without learning anything about the spiritual life. There is a world of difference between being a disciple and being a dabbler in religion. One is lightning and the other is a picture of lightning. The Roman Catholic Church must face the fact that we have among our members too many dabblers in religion, and not enough disciples.

I believe in infant baptism, but the Church has a problem in its hands. One of weaknesses of the Church is the assumption that the infant is, from the baptism ceremony on, forever a believer. We often assume that from cradle to grave. I have noticed, though, that in spite of the fact that parishioners may have been educated in Catholic schools and have sat in a Catholic church every Sunday of their lives, they often cannot answer even the simplest question about their own faith.

I think I first recognized this fact when I worked in the home missions down in central Kentucky. I even wrote a doctoral thesis on it. My job in those days was to help start two Catholic parishes in areas of Kentucky where Catholics had never lived. I was not trained to be a missionary. I had to learn on the job. What startled me most was that many of the Catholics who moved into these little parishes did not know enough about their own faith to be able to help establish that parish. Most of my time was spent teaching the basics of Christianity and the basics of Catholicism to that little parish.

I believe that the biggest challenge facing the Roman Catholic Church is how to help people make the transition from being Catholic Christians by birth to being Catholic Christians by choice — from becoming dabblers in religion to becoming intentional disciples of Jesus Christ. Surely you have noticed that the old system is collapsing. As a writer I came across recently put it, at some point in the distant past a decision was made that in the absence of internal acceptance of the Good News, external conformity would suffice. It is much easier to arrange for external conformity, to go through the motions of discipleship, than it is to be a disciple. During most of the Church's long history, external conformity was guaranteed by an elaborate system of sanctions and penalties, backed up by a glut of priests and sisters to enforce them. But these days, we are moving back where we started in the church. Discipleship is a matter of invitation and our response to that invitation will determine whether we are disciples. As I say in one of my mission talks, we will either choose Catholic Christianity, or we will lose it.

Fearful of allowing people to choose, some traditionalists in our church are still trying to figure out a way to force people to conform. In spite of their campaigns, Catholicism will either appeal to people today (especially the young) or it will be replaced with something else. If you don't believe me, go out the local mega-church and ask for a show of hands. There are hundreds of former Roman Catholics there. Sometimes as I think about that phenomenon, I wonder if it's a sign of their strength or of our weakness. But I do know one thing, that the Roman Catholic Church had better start preaching conversion and discipleship, and quit being so obsessed with conformity on the non-essentials. We need to figure out a way to convert large numbers of religious dabblers to discipleship, or we will not make it through this difficult time of transition. My fellow Catholics, it's either choose it or lose it! The old question was: "Do you know the answers in the catechism?" The new question is: "Do you believe the answers enough to live them?"

Peter the Apostle is, I believe, a perfect model for today's Catholics. In today's gospel (John 21:1-19) Peter was invited not once, but twice to follow Jesus. He received a second call. At the beginning of the Gospel, Peter answered Jesus' invitation to follow him. Peter walked behind Jesus, heard what Jesus taught, bragged a little bit about what he's going to do, but Peter failed to understand what Jesus meant. He missed the point over and over again, and finally crumbled when the heat was on. Many of us who were baptized as infants grew up being pumped full of religious facts. Our behavior was held in check by an elaborate system of rules and regulations. And since that old system began collapsing, I've heard lots of Catholics ask, "Father, am I losing my faith?"

We know all the religious words, but the real measure of discipleship is whether Jesus is alive in our hearts. Does he live where we make decisions? We may admire Jesus, may fear him, may remember the major events of his life but the crucial question is: Have we consecrated ourselves to him in partnership, as disciples? Disciples are dedicated to transforming their lives so that they can become as Jesus-

23

like as possible. Religious dabblers try to squeeze Jesus in somewhere, as long as he doesn't demand too much.

After the resurrection, Peter is called once again to follow Jesus. And this time, Peter surrenders completely. He begins to recall all that Jesus had said and finally Peter begins to understand. He wakes up. He doesn't just assent to a few facts about Jesus, Peter allows this risen Lord to live in his heart. When he allows the risen Lord to live inside his heart, Peter begins to act like Jesus in the world around him.

My fellow Catholics, we are being issued a second call. We have memorized a lot of facts. We've attended a lot of services. We have even given our money to the work of the church, but in these days, in the church as it is, we must consciously decide to become disciples, serious students of the Master, or we will continue to be dabblers in religion. We need to know that deciding to transform our lives is a lot like buying an exercise bicycle. Simply buying the bike doesn't take off any pounds, doesn't make our hearts stronger or make us one bit healthier. We still have to pedal on that thing and work up a lot of sweat. In discipleship, as in many other good things, the spirit may be willing but the flesh is always weak. That's why discipleship is a lifelong response, hour-by-hour, day-by-day, year-by-year until one day we wake up and realize that we have indeed moved closer to God. As disciples, we make God visible in the world around us and we are carrying out the work of God in today's world.

The challenge which I believe is facing millions of Roman Catholics is simply this: Will we answer the second call? Will we become enthusiastic, lifelong students of the Master? Do we have the guts to handle lightning, or will we settle for second-hand stories about people who have handled it. The future health of our church depends on how many of us are willing to make that leap. In the meantime, we had better start making more sense than we do now. We had better start preaching conversion, not just external conformity, or else we will end up looking more like the empty tomb than the risen Christ. This cannot be accomplished by a decree from the Vatican, only by the passionate discipleship of enough individual members. The words of Jesus are meant for us: Follow me!

May 3, 1992

Beliefs Are Not Enough

The Lord has been taken from the tomb! We don't know where they have put him! Remember, as yet they did not understand the Scripture that Jesus had to rise from the dead.

JOHN 20

———— ♥ ————

It wouldn't be Easter without confusion. To start with, this is the weekend we make the change to daylight savings time. There's no telling how many people will be late for Mass today, or miss it altogether. Second, there are guests in town and people have been trying to adapt to having two, three or four more people in an already congested house. Third, there are the new clothes that are inevitably too tight, too short, too long or too something. Finally, there are the crying children, high on chocolate, who insist on digging in their heels on almost everything.

It wouldn't be Easter without confusion. As today, so it was that first Easter morning. What started out as a peaceful early morning visit to a grave exploded into chaos. The tomb was empty. The body was gone. The authorities accused the disciples of snatching the body in the middle of the night, right out from under the noses of the cemetery guards. Some hysterical women, racing home from the cemetery, claimed they had actually spoken to Jesus. His grieving disciples were utterly shocked and confused, and did not know what to believe, where to go, or what to do.

Everybody agreed that the tomb was empty and the body was missing. But what did that mean? Slowly but surely, they came to understand and believe: Christ is risen from the dead! That conviction started with a woman, Mary Magdalene, then spread to John, to Peter, and on to the rest of the apostles, finally even to Thomas! That belief has slowly but surely reached across the centuries, from one believer to another, to those of us gathered here this morning. And so we gather to celebrate our Easter faith: Christ has died. Christ is risen. Christ will come again!

You do believe, don't you? But believe what? I suspect that many people who call themselves "Christians" believe (at best) in a mere resuscitation of the body, rather than the resurrection of the body. They believe that God somehow revived the dead body of Jesus. They believe that on Good Friday the lungs quit breathing, the heart stopped beating and the brain ceased to wave. And then, miracle of miracles, those lungs, heart and brain started up again on that first Easter Sunday! As miraculous as that might be, mere belief in a resuscitation of the body is not enough. There is a whole lot more going on here than that!

If we merely believe that the resurrection of Jesus was an historical event that occurred long ago (as hard as even that belief is to come to) it is simply not enough. Death and Resurrection is not just something to be believed and admired, it is a principle to be lived out. Death and Resurrection is not just an event, it is a way of living. Let me try to explain.

It is vitally important to remember that death was not forced on Jesus. It was a death that he "freely accepted," in the words the priest says over the bread at every Mass. It was a death that he "obediently accepted," as we read on Palm Sunday. It was a death that he "let be done" to him, as he prayed in the garden of Gethsemane. By embracing death freely, he triumphed over it. The lesson, the mystery, the life principle is simply this: Avoiding necessary pain leads to death and more pain, but embracing necessary pain leads to life and more life. Jesus explained it in agricultural terms. "Unless a grain of wheat dies, unless it is sacrificed by throwing it into the earth, it remains just a grain of wheat. But if it gives its life, if it is sacrificed to the ground, it produces thirty or forty grains of wheat." (John 12:24)

Something has to die before new life can come about. Recovering alcoholics and drug addicts know this. An old life has to die before a new life can come about. Parents know this. The day comes when parents must let go, dying to an old way of relating to their children so that a child's new adult life can be born. Young married couples know this. Part of their single, ego-centeredness has to die before a marriage partnership can develop. When an alcoholic holds onto his bottle, when a parent tries to hold onto a child, when married people still act single, when a farmer holds onto his seed corn, new life is impossible. "No pain, no gain!" That's the mystery of death and resurrection. That is the life principle that Jesus wants us to know and emulate. When we live this principle, Jesus Christ is no longer an historical figure, he is alive in our hearts. He dies and rises with us, over and over again, giving us new life over and over again. The secret to overcoming any problem facing us is to embrace the pain as the only way to conquer it. There is no way around it!

We cannot stop at having beliefs about Easter. We must have Easter faith. Easter cannot be understood. It has to be lived. When Jesus is alive in our hearts, we can face and embrace all the pain that life throws at us. By facing it and embracing it, we can triumph over it, even the pain of our

29

own deaths! The message of Easter is simply this: there is **always** new life on the other side of embraced pain, so reach out and hug it!

April 7, 1996

People With An Eye Out For God

After Jesus' birth in Bethlehem, astrologers from the East arrived in Jerusalem one day inquiring....

MATTHEW 2

------ ♥ ------

We will begin today with a short quiz on the gospel reading just to see if you were **really** paying attention. Are you ready? How many wise men visited the newborn Jesus? I hope you're not thinking "three," because if you are, you are just guessing! I realize that three gifts are listed, but it does not tell us how many wise men brought them! There may have been two, three, five, seven, ten, thirty or even fifty for that matter! Hey, they might have all chipped in to buy three nice presents, rather than bringing several cheap ones, who knows? Seriously, though, the text does not tell us how many there were. Popular medieval devotion deduced that there were three wise men from the number of gifts mentioned, then invented the names Caspar, Melchior and Bathasar for them, but these details have no biblical basis.

Besides, who cares? The story of the Magi is primarily theological in construct and purpose anyway. The writer of Matthew's gospel wants the reader to understand that even Gentiles, non-Jews, are included in God's love. This theme that Jesus was the Messiah who was accepted by the Gentiles and rejected by the Jews is found throughout the New Testament, but is especially emphasized in Matthew.

This year, I want to focus on these Magi characters,

however many there may have been! I am fascinated by these people whose profession it was to keep an eye out for God! The Magi had dedicated their lives to watching the heavens for signs from God. They were wise and holy men, priests really, who dedicated their lives to the pursuit of wisdom and truth. They were professional spiritual seekers.

Who were these strange people, anyway? In the original Greek, they are called *magos,* a word translated sometimes as "Magi," sometimes as "wise men," sometimes as "astrologers" and sometimes as "kings." They were probably members of a tribe of Persian priests, from the area we know as modern day Iraq. They were teachers and instructors of the Persian kings. They were men of holiness and wisdom, skilled in philosophy, medicine and natural science. In those days, everyone believed in astrology. It was these men's job to watch the heavens for anything peculiar. The heavens were so orderly that if something unusual happened, it was taken to mean that God was up to something or was about to make a special announcement. An especially brilliant star meant that some great king had been born. It may seem odd to us that people would "follow a star," setting out to find a king, but at the time of Jesus this could very well have happened. There was in the world at that time a strange feeling of anticipation that a king would come. An unusually brilliant star would have drawn great, great interest. People were waiting for God and the desire for God was in their hearts. In fact, historians tell us that between the years 5 BC and 2 BC, an unusual astronomical phenomenon occurred. On the first day of the Egyptian month *Mesori,* Sirius, the dog star, rose at sunrise and shone with extraordinary brilliance. *Mesori* means "the birth of a prince." This could very well have been the star that brought these "wise men" to Bethlehem!

I thought to myself the other day as I was writing this talk, "I wonder what it would be like to have a whole parish of "magi," people dedicated to a serious search for God, people who were driven to find out as much as they could about God, people who always had an eye on God, people who had dedicated themselves to the truth and to living by it?" Well, all we need is enough people who actually want it and commit to it. As James Allen puts it in his book *As You Think:* "To desire is to obtain; to aspire is to achieve."

"Ask and it will be given to you. Seek and you shall find. Knock and the door will be opened to you." (Matthew 7:7) I have reason to conclude that we already have a very high percentage of "magi" in our midst, and that the number is growing. You are hungry for spiritual and personal growth and you have found ways to feed yourselves. You are serious seekers. You, not the mean-spirited legalists, are the salvation of the Catholic Church. As far as I am concerned, "liberals" and "conservatives" are both wrong. We need neither religious robots nor spiritual marshmallows. We need "magi," wise and holy men and women who have an eye on God and who attract other people to become "magi" as well. This year, I challenge more of you to become "magi," serious spiritual seekers, people with an eye out for God!

January 7, 1996

Putting Out Into The Deep

Put out into the deep water.... Do not be afraid.

LUKE 5

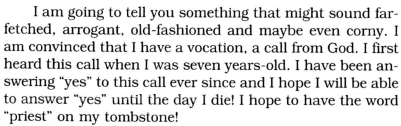

I am going to tell you something that might sound far-fetched, arrogant, old-fashioned and maybe even corny. I am convinced that I have a vocation, a call from God. I first heard this call when I was seven years-old. I have been answering "yes" to this call ever since and I hope I will be able to answer "yes" until the day I die! I hope to have the word "priest" on my tombstone!

God did not appear to me or send an angel to make a vocation pitch. God's invitation was placed in the mouth of my second grade teacher, Sister Mary Ancilla. She was going around the room one day, asking each student to tell the others what he or she wanted to be when they grew up. "What do you want to be when you grow up?" I remember, very clearly, the question, my answer, and how I felt about it.

"Do not be afraid," Jesus says to Peter when he calls him in today's Gospel. How appropriate! God asks for a lot of courage, even as he invites you to let go of fear. I remember how afraid I was to say the word "priest" in the second grade. I expected the other kids to tease me after class. (Hey! It's "Father Knott!") But I said it anyway: "I want to be a priest." I remember how afraid I was to leave home and family to enter the seminary at age thirteen. I remember how much courage it took to stay in seminary for twelve years, and I remember the courage it took to leave when I graduated. I remember how afraid I was when I left for my first assignment, the home missions; how afraid I was when I went deeper into mission work in my second assignment; how afraid I was when I went to Calvary, my third assignment; and especially how afraid I was when I first came here! "Do not be afraid?" Peter should have smelled a rat, right then and there!

Fear is normal after saying "yes" to God! But fear is not a valid reason to back off! A "called" person must overcome fear, not only at the beginning, but all along the way. A vocation is a faith-walk, not a cake-walk! To borrow a phrase from Luke's Gospel, a vocation always involves "putting out into deep water." It's not for people who insist on clinging to the safety of the shore, not for the faint of heart, not for spiritual cowards!

One day, as Peter was going about the business of washing his fishing nets and hanging them out to dry, a routine he had probably done every day of his life, Jesus invited him to "put out into deep water." Peter tried to evade the call by pleading unworthiness, by trying to convince Jesus that there were "no fish in his pond." It didn't work. The invitation had been made. A response, not excuses, was required. "Do not be afraid!" With that, Peter parked his boat on the shore forever and walked upon deep water the rest of his life, battling fear every step of the way! He failed sometimes, but he got back up and got back on the path.

You have a "vocation" too. Maybe you've never thought about it. Maybe you have never used that word. But **you** have a "vocation" too — be it marriage, religious life, parenthood, public service or whatever. A "vocation" is God's summons to move in a certain direction with your life. This call is heard in the heart, not necessarily in the ear, but it

36

must be heeded nevertheless. The phrase "follow your heart" may express it best. We are our happiest when we "follow our hearts." We are most unhappy when we don't. God's summons is the inner commitment to be true to ourselves and to follow our dreams and it triggers the help we need at the time we need it. There is a path for each of us. When we are on the right path, we know the next right action, even though we may not yet see what is just around the bend. By trusting, we learn that we can trust.

A "vocation" seems to follow a universal pattern — the call; the resistance; the call is repeated and help is offered; there is no peace until the call is accepted. We hear it in Jesus' call to Peter. "Peter, put out into the deep!" "Leave me, Lord. I am a sinful man." "Have no fear. I will make you a fisher of men." "He left everything and followed him." We hear it in God's call to Jeremiah. "Jeremiah, before you were born, I dedicated you and appointed you." "I am too young." "Have no fear. I am with you. I will put the right words in your mouth."

God calls. God knows we are afraid. God supplies what we need. Our own frustration will result if we resist! Our own happiness will result if we accept. This holds true for all vocations because to reject God's call is to reject who we are, who we were uniquely created to be. Our happiness and sanity are connected to our vocation.

I would like to conclude with a few words to our young members. Each of **you** has a vocation, an inner dream that will unfold and reveal itself if you just have the courage to listen and accept what it is. Train yourself to listen to your own heart. Acceptance is often difficult because it demands the courage to act. Very often just knowing what your vocation is will trigger resistance, but resistance leads to self-destruction. Following your hearts will lead to happiness.

37

Your truest dream for yourself is always God's will for you. God wants you to be happy. True happiness is not to be confused with pleasure-seeking. Being happy takes a lot of courage, a lot of trust, a lifetime of conquering your own fears, but do it. Your happiness is at stake.

You have a vocation. Listen for your call with your heart. Like Peter, when you hear it, drop everything else and follow it. Don't let fear hold you back. God not only calls you to this happiness; God is with you to help you as you respond to the call you hear. Who knows? Maybe somebody out there is even called to be a priest!

February 5, 1995

Stir Into Flame

I remind you to stir into flame the gift of God that you have through the imposition of my hands. For God did not give us a spirit of cowardice but rather of power and love and self-control.

2 TIMOTHY 1:6-7

———— ♥ ————

Last weekend, I got a chance to take a free trip to Montreal, Canada with a friend of mine, Fr. Stoltz. I had been saving frequent flyer points for the last five years and so we chose Montreal, a city neither of us had ever seen. We visited the Basilica of Notre Dame, a gorgeous, ornate old church whose blue ceiling is spangled with gold stars. It was much more ornate than this cathedral! This basilica looked like a carved wooden wedding cake with gold trim. There were numerous altars, shrines and confessionals around the sides and across the back. During the time we spent in the church, I saw one or two people trying to pray and close to a hundred gawking tourists, talking, snapping pictures and listening to guides explain the history of the place. As we were leaving, Joe turned to me and said, "The confessionals are empty and the church is a tourist attraction!" Like most of the old European churches I've visited, it struck me as an ornate monument to the living faith of dead saints and a noisy witness to the dead faith of many living people!

...stir into flame the gift of God bestowed when my hands were laid on you.

In our second reading today, Paul writes from a Roman prison cell as he awaits death by beheading. He writes to encourage his younger fellow missionary Timothy to stand firm in the faith in spite of adverse circumstances. In other words, Paul is essentially telling Timothy, "don't let the fire in your soul go out. As long as there is a single spark, you can fan it into flame once again." That spark, of course, is the gift of faith God bestowed on him when Paul baptized him. Obviously, Timothy's faith is beginning to break under the pressure. Paul counsels Timothy that, in the words of the gospel, "faith the size of mustard seed" can move mountains. Especially when things look bleak, Paul encourages Timothy to believe, in the words of the prophet Habakkuk, "the vision still has its time, presses on to fulfillment, and will not disappoint; if it delays, wait for it, it will surely come, it will not be late." (Habakkuk 2:3) This letter is all about enduring faith!

...stir into flame the gift of God bestowed when my hands were laid on you.

Most of us were baptized as infants. A mustard seed of faith was planted in our hearts and souls. It wasn't something we earned, something we deserved or a change of which we were even conscious. This seed of faith was a gift from a loving God! On that day, our parents and godparents were handed a lighted candle with these words, "This light is entrusted to you to be kept burning brightly. This child of yours has been enlightened by Christ. This child is to walk always as a child of light. May the child keep the flame of faith alive in his or her heart." The responsibility for nurturing that mustard seed of faith, protecting that light, fell on our parents and godparents until Confirmation, when the responsibility was turned over to us. Some of our parents did not accept their responsibility and let the flame almost die out in us. Others of us did not take responsibility for our own flame of faith and allowed it to almost go out. But a spark is still there, even if we have forgotten all about it. It has always been there waiting to be "fanned into flame." It will be there as long as we are alive!

When I became pastor here in 1983, I was asked to "do something with the Cathedral." These buildings were in bad shape, and a once thriving parish and school had, over the years, almost died out. The school had been closed in the 1950s and the parish in 1983 was a little over one hundred parishioners, mostly senior citizens. When I was asked to "do something" with the Cathedral, it never even entered my mind to renovate any buildings. I took the bishop's directive to mean "do something" about the Cathedral congregation! It was a little like the story of St. Francis who heard a voice say, "rebuild my church!" He first responded by renovating all the old church buildings he could find. Only later did St. Francis understood that voice to mean, "stir into flame the gift of faith in the hearts of church members." That's what "rebuilding the church" really means, raising spiritual awareness and encouraging growth in the people's hearts.

When I look out from this pulpit, I am both amazed and proud of what has happened around here in the last twelve years. Yes, the restored church building and refurbished rectory are beautiful! Yes, the gift shop is making money! Yes, the Arts and Music Program is excellent! Yes, we've raised a great deal of money.

But do you know what I am most proud of? You! This is not just another empty and beautiful tourist attraction! This

41

is the home of a living, breathing, active and deeply serious faith community! I have saved hundreds of letters over the last twelve years from people who have had their faith "fanned into flame" right here! Some have returned to the church after having been gone for twenty-five and fifty years! Many have never physically left the church, but they tell me they have experienced a personal, adult faith here for the first time in their lives. Still others have been attracted to the Catholic faith for the first time because of the health and hospitality of this community. The only thing I want to take with me when my time comes to leave are those letters because, no matter how bad things might be or how discouraged I might get, those letters will remind me that all the years I have spent here as a priest were well worth the effort!

My dear friends, I am very proud of you! I am very happy to be the pastor of so many spiritual seekers, people who go to great pains to get here Sunday after Sunday, people who are seriously trying to "fan into flame" the gift of faith bestowed on them in baptism. I have never experienced anything like this in my life! As a result, my own enthusiasm for the priesthood and for my Catholic Christian faith is stronger than it has ever been — in spite of the mess, confusion, pain and chaos we are going through as a church. This is a time of intense spiritual growth for me as well. I thank God for you and for your spiritual progress. We can inspire each other, but the bottom line is this: Each one of us is responsible for fanning our individual spark of faith in flame! What better place than this! What better time than now!

October 8, 1995

Led By The Spirit

If we live by the Spirit, let us also be guided by the Spirit.
GALATIANS 5

———— ♥ ————

A few years ago there was a popular country song with a line that went, "You're no longer in charge of my thinking." I believe the song was about a woman who was taking back control of her life from someone who had exercised tremendous negative power over her. "I'm sorry," she sings, "but you're no longer in charge of my thinking!" More than once that song caused me to stop and ask myself, "Just who is in charge of **your** thinking, Ronald? Who **really** calls the shots?" When I make life decisions, do I listen to the many confusing voices outside myself or to that small little voice within me? How much control does popular opinion, expedience, or habit have over me? In other words, do I take my cues for living from the inside or from the outside?

> *If we live by the Spirit, let us be guided by the*
> *Spirit.*

According to the gospel, Jesus appears on the public stage as a young man, after growing up in obscurity. Something impels him to go to a wilderness preacher named John. John adhered to a charismatic stream of the Judaism of his day. John's message to his Jewish audience was that it was not good enough simply to have Jewish blood, that

Jewish people had to have an intense relationship with God, one sealed by a ritual initiation — baptism. Crowds flocked to this charismatic preacher named John. Some underwent this baptism. Jesus was one of them. During his baptism, Jesus experienced the heavens being opened, like a door or a tear. He got a glimpse of heaven, the other real world in which we live, but cannot see. Through this tear, he experienced the Spirit descending upon him. From then on, Jesus was led by the Spirit. From then on, he took his cues from the Spirit. When he made life decisions, as he did for forty days in the desert, he tuned out all other voices, and tuned in to the voice of God. Fidelity to that inner voice became the foundation of all his life decisions for Jesus. He was "led by the Spirit." Indeed, this sequence of initiation into the world of the Spirit, followed by a testing or ordeal in the wilderness, is strikingly similar to what is reported by charismatic figures of all cultures, including Native Americans and their "vision quests."

Allowing ourselves to be led by the Spirit is very, very hard for people in our culture. The whole notion of a "world of the Spirit" is vague and suspect. The cultural tradition in which Jesus lived took for granted that there are both spiritual and material worlds which could be known at the same time. The "world of the Spirit" is not part of our contemporary, shared understanding of reality. We tend to see things in only one dimension. The realm of the visible and material is the only reality our culture acknowledges..

Jesus believed and taught that there is another realm in addition to the material and visible realm. He made contact with that realm at his baptism and then spent his life plugged into its power. That is what being "led by the Spirit" means. He stayed in contact with the "world of the Spirit" through prayer. It is true that Jesus said formal prayers with the community in the synagogue and with his family at the family table. But the kind of prayer I am speaking of here is that much more intense form of prayer in which Jesus engaged when he went off alone into the desert, up mountain sides, out into the garden or out onto the lake. This prayer is characterized by internal silence and lengthy periods of solitary time. In this state, he entered into deeper levels of consciousness. He entered the realm of the Spirit and experienced God. At the end of that prayer, he felt guided and strengthened for living in the material and visible world.

The reason so many cannot not allow themselves to be "led by the spirit," is that they have not yet made contact with the "world of the spirit." These people may still be saying prayers and hoping for an afterlife, but religion doesn't make much sense to them. They are usually pretty good people and may try hard to do the right thing, but their religion has no power in it. In years past, guilt kept many in church. Now that guilt is scarce, many no longer have any personal desire to be seriously connected to the religion of their upbringing. It is the duty of religion to teach people about this other world, to offer opportunities for making connections, and to support those who are plugged into it. Sadly, many never get beyond the forms of religion. Rather than religion being a source for powerful living, it is simply something to be endured until the big "poof" in an afterlife. How sad!

Today we celebrate Pentecost, that day when the early disciples made contact with the "world of the Spirit," a contact that would become a conduit of power for heroic living. As we read about them after Pentecost, the phrases "guided by the Spirit," "led by the Spirit" and "under the power of the Spirit" are part of the story of everything they did.

45

How about you? Who is in charge of your thinking? From whom do you take cues for living your life? Do you take cues from the many noisy voices outside yourself, or from that small, quiet voice within yourself? Are you "led by the Spirit?" The good news today is that you are already initiated into the Spirit world. You were initiated into that world at your baptism and confirmation. The Spirit is already within you, waiting to help you, if you are willing to be led by the Spirit. Like a seed waiting for water to spring to life, the Spirit is waiting for your cooperation. Therefore, we need not so much pray that the Holy Spirit will come, but rather that we might wake up to the Spirit who is already within us. Let us pray that the Spirit will open our minds and hearts so that we can not only experience the presence of God, but also direct our daily lives from that awareness. Believe me, being led by the Spirit is a lot more rewarding than being led around by the nose by knee-jerk reactions to what everyone else is doing!

May 18, 1997

On the Way to a New Heart: The Adventure of Doing Your Part

— ❤ —

Taking Charge Of Your Own Spiritual Transformation
Part 1: Choose It Or Lose It !

If you choose, you can keep the commandments.
Before you are life and death,
Whichever you choose shall be given to you.

SIRACH 15

———— ♥ ————

On one of her trips to the United States, Mother Teresa of Calcutta said, "The poverty in America is much worse than the poverty of India: It's spiritual!" Jesse Jackson has said that most of our social problems have at their root a "spiritual crisis." Vaclav Havel of the new Czech Republic told Congress in 1990 that "nothing will change for the better until we have a global revolution of moral consciousness."

Surely you know that a lot of things are breaking down in the culture around us. The creed the world lives by at the moment will just not do! In this country each year we have five thousand teenage suicides and many more runaway children. We have forty-five thousand deaths on our roadways, a major crime every two seconds and an unknown number of people addicted to alcohol, tranquilizers and other drugs. One out of five American children lives in poverty and millions are victims of a sickening pattern of neglect and abuse which is producing children who are inwardly isolated and emotionally unapproachable. They have been described as "children without a conscience." Some say fifteen percent of the population may be afflicted with some degree of "attachment disorder" that erupts into violence and destruction. New laws and expensive programs don't seem to be making much of a dent in the problem. There seems to be an agreement evolving that these problems cannot be fixed from the outside.

The good news is this: There is an increased yearning for something spiritual now that materialism has proved unsatisfying. Humankind may have turned the corner, finally realizing that the material world is only part of reality. We are re-discovering that healing is not something bestowed on us from outside, but something which originates from deep within each human person. We are beginning to pay at least as much attention to our spiritual lives as we do to our hair. Sick and tired of being sick and tired, maybe we are now ready to pay more attention to building ourselves from the inside out! That's what this series of homilies is all about: Teaching the necessity and a method for building ourselves from the inside out!

Surely you know that there are a lot of things breaking down in the church as well. Church authorities rant and rave that Catholics ought to listen to them, but their words seem to have less and less effect. The fundamentalists of our church have tried to tighten the rules and stiffen the sanctions, to little avail. (I read somewhere that the last, desperate act of any dying organization is to come out with a new edition of the rules.) What is wrong with the Church cannot be fixed from the outside. After centuries of having religious discipline imposed on us, enforced by a system of sanctions that made sure the discipline was followed, we surely realize by now that the system has collapsed. There isn't anyone around any more to **make** us be religious or be Catholic. We will either freely choose it or we will lose it, no matter how many new catechisms are published in Rome!

Catholics, from now on spiritual discipline will not come from rule book-wielding authority figures, but from within each one of us! From now on we will be Catholic by choice, not by circumstance. We will choose it or lose it! Our church is being renewed, but what's wrong cannot be fixed from the outside. It is being fixed from the inside out, one person at a time!

The Church has a gold mine of spiritual wisdom at its disposal, but instead of focusing on the spiritual transformation that is at the heart of the Jesus' message, the Church keeps getting mired down. Sometimes the Church seems more interested in promoting **conform**ation (obedience to authority), **reform**ation (an obsession with the forms of religion) and **inform**ation (the transmission of facts). Theologian Charles Curran put it this way: "Jesus is direct, straightforward, simple; and yet Christian teaching and preaching today is too often legalistic in tone. People are warned to do this, to avoid that. The emphasis falls on a particular action or mode of external conduct. The authentic Christian message, however, calls above all for a change of heart; a radical, internal change of the person. External actions will follow from the person's changed heart. The gospel reminds us that a good tree will bring forth good fruit and the evil tree will bring forth evil fruit. (Mt. 7:17-20). The Christian message aims to produce the good tree from which comes good fruit. If a person changes his heart, then his actions will change accordingly."

It may sound odd to you, but Alcoholics Anonymous, not the Church, seems to be leading the way in teaching spiritual growth. Alcoholics Anonymous and other Twelve

51

Step programs have given us a popular model for personal and spiritual transformation. The adventure of going inside ourselves and the agony of breaking through in our awareness of God, ourselves and others is the work of spiritual growth and transformation. Fixing the world begins "in here," not "out there." "It is easier to put on slippers than it is to carpet the world!"

I invite you to explore the possibility of committing yourself to some serious spiritual transformation as you read the five talks that follow. I'm not talking about adding more pious practices to your schedule, but about going inside yourself for a thorough examination. I'm talking about becoming your own spiritual director, about becoming the pilot of your own happiness, about a partnership with an incredibly loving God who is so eaten up with love for us that He had an only Son become one of us!

Many of us who grew up in the old Church have spent years and years pursuing freedom from our religious heritage. Now we have the freedom to choose it, to be nourished by it, and to live in its beauty and strength. When we have made that passage, we will find ourselves transformed. A new mind and a new heart will make our worlds new. When enough of us are transformed, we will wake some day and realize that the whole world has been transformed around us!

This parish community has already entered one of those transforming processes. Look around you! With the beginning of the work of restoration this building will change day by day, and we will be changed along with it. We cannot go back to what we had last week. The old and the familiar are passing away. We will need to be spiritually strong if we are going to be courageous enough to embrace the new, and trust enough to let go of what used to be! I will use this experience as a pattern to talk about our individual spiritual and personal transformations, so that when this building sparkles again, materially; so will we, spiritually!

February 14, 1993

Taking Charge Of Your Own Spiritual Transformation
Part 2: Resistance To The Call To Holiness And Wholeness

In a word, you must be perfected as your heavenly Father is perfect.

MATTHEW 5

———— ♥ ————

In June, 1979, I graduated from McCormick Presbyterian Seminary in Chicago with a Doctor of Ministry degree in Parish Revitalization. Our graduation ceremony was held at the Rockefeller Chapel on the campus of the University of Chicago. The commencement speaker was the pastor of Ebenezer Baptist Church in Atlanta. His text was the creation story of Genesis. I never will forget his summary of that great biblical treasure. "God has always been happy being God. The animals have always been happy being animals. Human beings have never been happy being human beings. They want to be God one day and animals the next!"

Human beings have never been happy being who God created them to be! They have either wanted to be like God, more than they are, or like animals, less than they are! But holiness is about becoming who we **really** are, no more and no less! The path to holiness leads through many layers of resistance. Spiritual transformation is about "breaking through" all within us that resists our awareness of God, ourselves and each other! Spiritual transformation is about waking up to who we are — precious and unique children of God! Spiritual transformation is about standing up to all the self-deception within us and all the lies around us.

Holiness is about accepting who we are — no more and no less. Adam and Eve were ashamed of who they were because they compared themselves to God. Instead of celebrating their humanity, comparing themselves to God made them feel weak, bad, imperfect, wrong, unsuccessful and not what they should be. John Jacob Raub, a Trappist monk at Gethsemani, suggests that when God questions Adam — "Who told you that you were naked?" — we are meant to hear "Who told you that you were bad? Who told you that you were separated from me?" The work of spiritual transformation is the work of cutting through all the lies, excuses, hiding and shame that we produce from inside, or absorb from others on the outside!

Why do we resist becoming who we are? Why do we run from it, drug it, deny it and hide from it? We resist, first of all, because we are lazy. Resistance to becoming who we really are is an alibi for not taking responsibility for the goodness in us. If we convince ourselves that we have nothing to give, then we are excused from giving. If we convince ourselves that we are not good enough, then we are exempt from trying anything new. If we convince ourselves that we are nothing, then no one can expect anything **but** nothing from us! No one, after all, can blame us for throwing away what is worthless.

Why do we resist becoming who we are? We are afraid that God might want to take away our idols, drugs, excuses, denials and lies. We are afraid that God may want to take from us what we are loath to part with, to ask of us what we are not ready to give up. We fear what God might demand of us if we let God in. We don't want God roaming through our messy houses. We bar the doors. God wants to fill our emptiness to the brim. God waits for our permission to enter, our willingness, our openness to receive.

This self-hating image of ourselves is a lie we project onto God. We think God feels about us the same way we do about ourselves, so we bar the door. We set limits on God's largesse. This self-alienation results in a feeling that we are separated not only from ourselves but also from God. It's a lie! It's an imagined gap! To live with it, we must hide, pretend, numb ourselves and isolate! God patiently waits for us to wake up and let go of this self-alienation. The journey home is the work of spiritual transformation. The goal of the journey is becoming what we truly are, beloved sons and daughters of God!

Personal and spiritual suicide is the result of saying "no" to opportunities to grow. There moves within us both the drive to go forward and the urge to hold back, operating simultaneously. When we give in to the urge to hold back, we commit personal and spiritual suicide. When we commit to the process of transformation, we grow and thrive. Resistance is that subtle inner mechanism that urges us to back off from life's difficulties and demands. Most unhappy people are basically cowards who seek comfort rather than doing battle with the "demons" within them and in the world around them. A truly whole individual will not tolerate his/her own resistance. Resistance is often rooted in fear of change in the *status quo* or in fear of losing what we have. Resistance is motivated by fear. The basis of fear is laziness, a pervasive pattern of refusal to take responsibility for acting — for **doing** something.

Resistance is something we each learned as a child.

When a child encounters something he does not want, he has all kinds of maneuvers to avoid it, like crying, hiding or fighting. Unless we are taught, or learn to teach ourselves to face our problems directly and work through them, the patterns of resistance will be repeated until they become natural, accepted ways to act. When we act out our patterns of resistance, we slowly commit spiritual and personal suicide. Rather than tackling our resistance and transforming it, we waste an awesome amount of energy making sure we are asleep, making sure we don't know, while whatever monster we are avoiding gets bigger and bigger. Resistance settles for chronic dull pain rather than brief, acute confrontation. Cowards, spiritual and personal, feed on it!

God invites us to the risky adventure of spiritual and personal transformation. That's what Jesus meant when he challenged us to "invest our talents." When we take that risk, we double those talents. When we back off, we lose what little we have. In the folk story Hansel and Gretel, it is not until they get up enough nerve to enter the old hag's house that the children find pearls and precious stones in every room. Resistance produces death. Courage produces life.

We have the capacity to deny or mask our pain, or to transform it by paying attention to it. The only way out of pain is through it. There is healing magic in attention. There is chronic, dull pain in avoidance. Those who discover this phenomenon gradually realize that the reward is worth the scariness of being wide awake in the face of life!

God calls us to holiness. Holiness is really another word for wholeness. God calls us to quit hiding, quit blaming, quit denying and masking who we really are! God calls us to be whole and happy, gives us all we need to accomplish it, but leaves us free to accept this adventure or reject it.

But we have to know that personal and spiritual suicide is the result of saying "no" while health and happiness are the results of saying "yes." This adventure is not for cowards, because once the quest has begun, there are "dragons to be slain" before the "treasures" can be claimed!

February 21, 1993

Taking Charge Of Your Own Spiritual Transformation
Part 3: Entering The Narrow Door

Jesus was led into the desert by the Spirit to be tempted by the devil.

MATTHEW 4

———— ♥ ————

THE most significant event of my life, even more significant than being ordained, happened in the spring of 1965. I was extremely bashful. I avoided meeting new people or getting myself into unfamiliar situations. I was scared of life. I was what George Bernard Shaw called "a feverish little clod of grievances and ailments, complaining that the world would not dedicate itself to making me happy." I was standing on a fire escape outside my room at St. Meinrad Seminary with a fellow seminarian, Pat Murphy. In what had to be a moment of grace, an impulse gift from God, I suddenly blurted out, "Pat, I am so sick and tired of being bashful and scared of life that I'm going to do something about it even if it kills me!"

I was shocked by the words that came out of my mouth! But from that moment on, I have been standing up to the coward in me. I have been deliberately "slaying dragons" and "confronting demons" in my head and on my path ever since! I would not be standing here today if that "moment of grace" had not happened. I decided that day that I would not indulge my resistance to personal and spiritual growth anymore. I finally learned a fundamental lesson — fear and pain do not excuse backing off from life!

That day on the fire escape, I made my first conscious decision to enter the world of deliberate living! How appropriate and symbolic that the decision was made on a "fire escape!" Up to that point, my life had been guided by the belief that "life is something that happens to you and all you can do is make the most of it." From that day on, I have come to understand that pain serves a purpose. Pain captures our attention and lets us know that change is necessary. Pain signals that is time to move on and learn new behaviors. Unfortunately, many of us sabotage the possibility of growth by denying, numbing or backing away from the pain. We live in a culture that incessantly tells us that pain is to be avoided at all costs! This is where "following the crowd" is deadly, for there is no spiritual and personal health without embracing good pain. The wise know when pain must be embraced. Fools run from any hint of it!

Jesus embraced this kind of eye-opening experience at his baptism. In that moment of grace, Jesus realized where he was being called, and he committed himself to the path that would take him there! His "desert experience" is actually a preview of what lay ahead — demons! We need not be too literal here. "Demons" can be those voices we all hear in our heads that say "back off," "take the easy way," "be comfortable" and "don't know!" No sooner had Jesus made the commitment to walk his path, than these ""demons" went into action! But the gospel says he "cast out demons." Jesus walked right through death itself to claim victory. It is by "walking in his footsteps," by facing our demons down, that we, too, will triumph over them. There is "new life" awaiting each victory.

How does one "enter" this transforming process? Put most simply, you must change the way you interpret the things that happen to you. You must undergo radical "eye" surgery. Let me explain.

The entry point could be anything that shakes your present world to the foundation; a heart attack, a divorce, a death, a serious illness, major surgery or sudden unemployment. The entry point might also be some unplanned encounter; a new book, an adult education course, a new acquaintance or maybe a song or sermon! It doesn't make a bit of difference whether the event was self-initiated, circumstantial or forced upon you. It is your attitude toward the experience that counts. If you embrace the experience, growth is possible. If you reject the experience, a little more of yourself withers away! These events are rocks that come through the windows of every person's life. The message attached reads: "Opportunity is knocking." All each of us has to do is keep making positive responses to every invitation.

There are numerous ways to respond to these "rocks" that come crashing into our lives. Some people respond to their "entry event" with the curiosity of children. This is the response Jesus advocates. "Unless you become like a child (curious), you will not enter the reign of God." I have, over the years, observed people who respond this way. They are the widows who have many good, long cries and then one day courageously set out to create a new life! They are the amputees who push themselves to compete in the athletic world! They are the millions of AA members who celebrate their sobriety! One day a "rock" broke into their world and somehow they got that spark of courage necessary to say "yes" to its invitation to change. They stood up to all the "demons" who tried to dissuade them!

Another way to respond to an "entry event" is to run. Those who respond this way are often people who are afraid of having to let go of some favorite old habits, afraid of losing control, afraid of having to revise their maps of reality, afraid of all the work change will take. Instead of focusing their energies on finding the opportunity in this new situation, those who run waste their energies on resisting an unwanted reality. They think to themselves, "If I just don't like this enough, maybe it will go away." These are the people who go through life fine-tuning their impressive list of reasons for not being happy: "If this had not happened...," "if it weren't for him or her...," "if it weren't for the times we live in...," "You see, I have all these excuses for being unhappy. I'm a victim of circumstances!"

One final example of the way numerous people respond to these "entry events" is hesitation. Some people hesitate because of concern about how significant people might react should they seriously start to change. Sometimes lack of curiosity is used as a defense. As much as we like to complain, we really don't want things to be all that different! "What if I might have to become committed to some demanding discipline? What if I find out that what I really want out of life is radically different from what I have? What if I get 'caught up' in something, started having weird new experiences and worse yet, even grow to like them?"

We both fear and crave becoming ourselves — being who we really are! Somewhere at each entry point each person has to make a decision. You can say "no." Those with second thoughts can exit at any time. But if you say "yes," then things will never be quite the same. You are on your way to becoming a new person.

You have had these "rocks" come crashing into your

life many times, whether you recognized what they were or not! They may have been extremely painful, even tragic, events. They may have been mind-blowing "eureka" experiences. How did you respond to them? How are you responding to them? If you are ready for the adventure of spiritual and personal transformation, wrap your arms around the next one and see where it takes you. Put some passion into your search! You can become a new person as many times as you like, depending on how much courage you can muster and how much attention you can pay!

February 28, 1993

Taking Charge Of Your Own Spiritual Transformation
Part 4: It Never Stays The Same

The Lord said to Abram: "Go forth from the land of your kinsfolk to a land I will show you. Abram went as the Lord directed him. Abram was seventy-five years old when he left....

GENESIS 12

———— ♥ ————

It was about this time of year a decade ago when Archbishop Kelly pulled me aside at a priests' meeting and dropped these words on me: "I want you to come up to the Cathedral and do something with it! I'll give you a week or two to think about it." Talk about a "rock" crashing through the windows of my life! I was a very happy country pastor of about one hundred and fifty families. I was only three years into a ten year assignment. I was comfortable and loved. The people were fabulous. It was a piece of cake!

I was completely stunned by the invitation! My mind was immediately inundated with negative chatter. "Why give up my cozy little parish in the country for an aging old landmark in downtown Louisville?" The Cathedral had only a handful of parishioners, a bag full of problems and very little money! What could realistically be done downtown besides hold Masses? The expectations are unrealistic! I'll just say "no!" But along with that loud negative mind chatter was a small little voice in the back of my head which kept saying "Try it! You might just be able to do something! You will always regret it if you don't. You'll never know till you've tried it!" This "rock" was clearly marked "opportunity." I chose to listen to the small voice rather than the noisy mind chatter. After a few days, I wrote to the Archbishop and said "yes."

By the time I arrived in June, I was fired up! I had two associate pastors and an engraved invitation from the Archbishop himself to be as creative as I wanted to be! My enthusiasm was short lived. All my ideas took money. The only money the Cathedral had was in savings. We depended on tourists to pay the bills. The Chancery was afraid we would soon go through all our savings, so they were reluctant to release what we had!

I was so frustrated at the end of the first year that I wrote a letter threatening to resign unless I got more cooperation. The savings were released so that we could invest in some "people programs," especially music and liturgy. The Cathedral Heritage Foundation was created later in response to my plea for help in the awesome task of revitalizing the Cathedral. Gradually the parish started to grow. The Cathedral Heritage Foundation took off! Things began to click! Each year of experimentation and exploration of new ideas produced results. Yes, we had set-backs and frustrations, but as we enter the "big breakdown before the big breakthrough," I can smell a dream coming true! I think we're going to make it, if we just hang in there a little while longer. We will have our revitalized congregation and our restored facilities! Then, when the renovation of the Cathedral church is finished, we will have to display a new kind of courage and imagination if we are to use it well, harvesting its potential as a community-wide spiritual feeding center! For me this whole adventure has been a personal spiritual transformation process, and a communal process of growth we have shared as a parish!

The beautiful story of Abram's call from our first reading today (Genesis 12:1-4) is perfect for this homily's subject! At seventy-five a "rock" came crashing into Abram's life. He and Sarah were comfortably retired, almost with one foot in the grave! Can't you just hear what was going on in Abram's head? "You want me to be a father for the first time, now? You want me to re-locate, now? I must be crazy for even giving it a second thought! What kind of crazy old man would say yes to something like that? Sarah, pack the suitcase! Buy some maternity clothes! Put on your walking shoes and follow me!"

The Gospel today (Matthew 17:1-9) presents us with another perfect story on spiritual transformation. I call it a "glimpse of glory." Jesus gives his disciples a preview, a taste, a glimpse of the glory to come! Like most people in the initial stages of transformation who get a first glimpse of what is to come, Peter wants to bottle it! "Hey, this is so good, let's just stay up here forever!" But the disciples had only a glimpse! To get from "here" to "there" they had to descend into the valley of death and climb back out! Jesus meant for the preview, the taste, the glimpse to sustain them during the rough times on the journey.

We might call the second stage of spiritual and personal transformation the *exploration* stage. After saying yes to that "rock" that comes crashing into our lives, inviting us to growth and change, we set out (warily or enthusiastically) on an exploration phase. Having sensed there is something worth finding, we leave one shore and set sail for another. No longer resisting or fighting the process, our mind courageously opens up to receive the new! An open mind is essential before anything can change. With this new openness, the adventure begins!

In the exploration phase, the seeker, sooner or later, gets a taste of the world to come and, liking the taste, is like a kid in a candy store. Like Peter in Matthew's account of the transfiguration, we want to make the taste permanent! Your initial taste, your first success, is so empowering that you enter a period of "busy seeking." On one hand you experience exhilaration. You can't get enough of the new technique, teacher or program! You keep seeking to duplicate the initial, powerful experience! On the other hand, you also feel loneliness.

In this phase, you can become an obnoxious evangelist, driven to tell the whole world of your newly discovered cure for all ills! You know these people, those who've gone off to some monastery, shrine or program, had a charismatic experience, then returned home to unceasingly recruit new candidates for the experience while considering "going into it full time," all in a six month period! This period of "obnoxious certainty" often masks a craving for others to validate this powerful individual experience! This is Peter the Fisherman, bragging one minute and falling on his face the next.

If you don't burn out during this stage, or drive others crazy, you are ready to go deeper. The essential thing in this stage is not to give up, but to graduate! Graduating is about moving away from one point of view to finding a viewing point. You realize there is no single system that works for everybody, and so you concentrate on **your** path and allow others to find their own best way. From such a viewing point, you can appreciate not only our own point of view, but also many others at the same time.

Let me summarize the stages of spiritual and personal transformation I've discussed so far. In stage one, a "rock" marked "opportunity" breaks through the windows of your life. You look at the **entry point** and either reject its invitation to growth and change, or decide to embrace this opportunity. If you go with it, you enter stage two, **exploration.** In this stage, you often have very powerful, moving experiences through which you get a glimpse of what is to come. These experiences can be almost narcotic, making you a little "nuts." That's OK. It's part of the process. If you are patient with yourself and realize what it is (just a sample) you won't despair when it isn't permanent and you discover that there is still a lot of hard work to be done. You are ready to move into the next phase, **integration**.

The transfiguration story from today's gospel is very helpful to those in the second stage of spiritual and personal transformation. It reassures them that there is a place for these intense religious and personal growth experiences. But you cannot stay on the summit forever; you have to come down again. So why bother in the first place? Because that which is above knows what is below, but what is below does not know what is above. One climbs, one sees, one descends; one sees no longer, but one has seen!

In the transformation process, we often get glimpses of what is to come, just like we did when the community space downstairs was finished or when the sample window bay was completed in the church, but in between these glimpses there is a lot of hard, dirty work to be done before we can realize our dream. But these "mountain top" experiences can keep us going through the rough times. We can live by what little we have seen!

March 7, 1993

Taking Charge Of Your Own Spiritual Transformation
Part 5: Verification — No Second-hand God

No longer does our faith depend on your story. We have heard for ourselves, and we know that this really is the Savior of the world.

JOHN 4

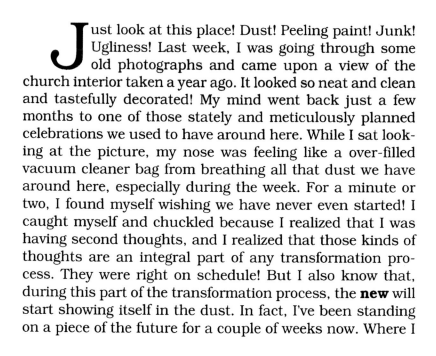

Just look at this place! Dust! Peeling paint! Junk! Ugliness! Last week, I was going through some old photographs and came upon a view of the church interior taken a year ago. It looked so neat and clean and tastefully decorated! My mind went back just a few months to one of those stately and meticulously planned celebrations we used to have around here. While I sat looking at the picture, my nose was feeling like a over-filled vacuum cleaner bag from breathing all that dust we have around here, especially during the week. For a minute or two, I found myself wishing we have never even started! I caught myself and chuckled because I realized that I was having second thoughts, and I realized that those kinds of thoughts are an integral part of any transformation process. They were right on schedule! But I also know that, during this part of the transformation process, the **new** will start showing itself in the dust. In fact, I've been standing on a piece of the future for a couple of weeks now. Where I stand is not a temporary platform. It **is** the front tip of the framework for the new altar steps and platform. Like a crocus sticking its head out of the snow, the restored cathedral will evolve from all this mess!

The perfect map for spiritual and personal transformers is, of course, found in our first reading, the Book of Exodus! (Exodus 17:3-7) In that story, the "people of God" find themselves enslaved in a foreign country. This is all of us when life isn't working. Moses proposes to lead them out to a "new land," into a new way of living. Moses is symbolic of the "rock marked opportunity" that comes crashing into our lives. The people of God decided to follow Moses and accepted the invitation to move into a new way of living. But like all people in a transformation process, their enthusiasm turned to despair when the trip had barely begun. Suddenly that old life began to look good in comparison to the discomfort of the "in between world," symbolized by the desert. Like all people in a transformation process, Moses' followers begin to regret ever having "set out." From time to time along the way to the Promised Land, a few tidbits of hope seem to come out of nowhere — some water, some strange-tasting bread and even a few quail. They continued in spite of the desert, only to realize one day that things suddenly began to get a little greener all the time! Then finally, they make it! "Land ho! Can't you see it, ever so faint, on the horizon there!" They finally move into the new life they used to dream about.

This is what should be expected in every spiritual and personal transformation! The steps are as certain as that spring follows winter. It's the way things work!

(1) You get an opportunity to change, an invitation to growth. If you refuse to tolerate your own resistance, but rather accept this opportunity, be it painful or pleasant,

you enter the process. You set out, optimistic that you can reach success by way of a slightly uphill path. You enter the process fueled with confidence.

(2) Not too long into the process, "demons" jump around in your head or onto your path to frustrate your plans and trip you up. They try to make you lose sight of your goal or convince you that you have fallen into a hopeless situation. This is precisely where we all sink or swim in the transformation process! No guts, no glory! Just because things are not turning out as you planned does not mean you should give up! This simply forces you to turn to your creative source and find an alternative way to get to your goal. Frustration is a necessary component of the transformation process. Do not make the mistake of giving up on your aspiration if you encounter what appears to be an impasse. Your response to this imagined impasse is what is truly important.

Many exit the process here. That's what all that whining is about in our first reading: they want to go back! "Why did you ever make us leave Egypt? Was it just to have us die here with thirst ... !" If you expect and face such situations and hold your ground in your own transformation, you will begin to see solutions you never thought of! All people in the process of spiritual and personal transformation find themselves in the shoes of the Israelites at some point or another. Things did not turn out as they had envisioned, but somehow things were turning out! Unfortunately, you may have to go through several of these episodes during this phase. This is the stage marked with dissonance, sharp conflict, oscillation and testing. In triumphing over all the temptations to give up, go back and quit, another step opens up in the process.

(4) Breakthroughs and insights begin to pop like corn! They might come with a jolt of amazement or a simple quiet

knowing! Before you know it, you actually become the new person you set out to be! This is the period of new strength and sureness! This is the next step after all the messes, setbacks and frustration. This is what we will see evolving from the dust and destruction we see around us. This will come, as surely as the spring will follow the winter. This is how it works, whether you are transforming a building or transforming yourself! The breakdown is the surest sign that a breakthrough is imminent. Pain is not a good reason to exit the process. It is the best reason to stay in it! Pain and chaos should come as no surprise in any transformation! In fact, it should be expected — you should plan on it!

Having survived one of these trips, you end up back on level ground, enjoying your triumph, living in your new world or being your changed self. And after you have survived a couple of these trips, you may find that you no long need "the program," "the guru" or the "leader:" you no longer need to trust them. When you have experienced for yourself that the process works you will trust it enough to apply it to other areas of your life. You trust your own inner "guru." You need less and less external validation. You are like the people of Samaria in today's Gospel who said: "No longer does our faith depend on your story. We have heard for ourselves, and we know that this really is the Savior of the world." (John 4:40-42)

Once you have been through the process a few times, you begin to understand how it works. You know that each time you apply the process to some area of your life which isn't working or you want to change, you will inevitably go through an unsettling period of disillusionment — temporarily throwing you into confusion and discomfort. You learn to expect it, and you ride this period out, knowing that victory is also inevitable! Here, the words of the Prophet

Habakkuk come to mind: "For the vision still has its time, presses on to fulfillment, and will not disappoint; if it delays, wait for it, it will surely come, it will not be late." (Habakkuk 2:3)

Having discovered how transformation works — having mastered the process, you are finally ready to start "throwing rocks through your own windows." You are ready to induce your own labor pains of growth and set out on one journey after another. Instead of being driven to accumulate more and more material benefits for yourself, your real love and passion in life will be for going deeper and deeper into yourself! Then you will have found the "pearl of great price," "the narrow door" and the kind of "wealth" that "moths cannot consume, rust cannot corrode and thieves cannot steal."

March 14, 1993

Taking Charge Of Your Own Spiritual Transformation
Part 6: Throwing Rocks Through Your Own Windows

"You are not counting us in with the blind, are you?" To which Jesus replied: "If you were blind there would be no sin in that. 'But we see,' you say, and your sin remains."

JOHN 9

———— ♥ ————

I cannot remember "the hour I first believed." But it seems to me that I have given my heart and soul to religion for as long as I can remember. I can still remember clearly struggling to memorize the Our Father and Hail Mary when I was six years old. The idea of becoming a priest came to me when I was seven years old. I joined the seminary at age thirteen years old. I was ordained at twenty-six years old. I was thirty-one years old when I became pastor of my first church; thirty-six years old when I became pastor of my second church. I was thirty-nine years old when I became pastor here at the Cathedral. I will be forty-nine years old next month! It seems that I have given my heart and soul to religion my whole life long.

While I would not trade my vocation with anybody, I am well aware that being a priest these days is not easy. I have watched most of my classmates leave the priesthood.

I have been embarrassed by the constant stream of scandals in which other priests have been involved, while I realize that "there, but for the grace of God, go I." I have spent a mountain of energy trying to heal the damage institutional religion has done to some people, while I tremble to think that a slip-up of mine could cause another "to lose their faith." I have worked with one hand to make a place for the rejected and marginalized in our church, while I work with the other hand to bandage my own wounds and keep myself from coming unglued. I continue to speak a message of hope to people who are a step or two away from giving up, while fighting off the urge to quit myself! It takes a special kind of courage to stay in organized religion today. On a bad day, I am tempted to believe that there are only two kinds of people left in the church today — the sound asleep and the heroic saintly. "We walk by faith and not by sight."

It pains me very much to see the church I have loved all my life undergoing so much trauma. But whether we like it or not, the old is passing away before our eyes. This has led many people to conclude, wrongly, that religion is dying. In response, conservatives are trying to drag us back to the "fleshpots of Egypt," which they imagine were the "good old days." But conservatives are learning that "those who try to preserve their lives will lose them even more." The ranting and raving about how they ought to be listened to is having less and less effect. They see "conformation," obedience to authority, as the answer. They even think they can get that obedience merely by demanding it. Liberals are no help either because they see the solution in more "reformation," the reorganization of religious forms. Iconoclasm, the careless destruction of religious symbols, is the agenda of some liberal religionists. Both conservatives and liberals are overcome with discouragement these days because they both miss the point. They are both obsessed with external fixes.

Religion is not dying, it is moving inside people and that is hard to track with polls that measure external religious behavior patterns. For that very reason, I am extremely hopeful and optimistic. Both conservatives and liberals miss the point: what's wrong with us cannot be fixed from the outside. They have both forgotten that the authentic Christian message calls first of all for a change of heart, a radical internal change of the person. Obedience to authority and structural reform is not a means, but an outcome, of transformation! External actions will follow from a person's changed heart! Most religious authorities and political leaders haven't figured this out yet! The interiorization of religion can neither be legislated nor demanded.

This series of homilies has been about fixing things from the inside out, not the other way around. This "blindness" which results from focusing on changing things "outside" is what keeps us wallowing in despair and ineffectiveness. It is precisely from this "blindness" that Jesus invites us to be healed! Life does not unwind from the outside inward, but from the inside outward. When we make this transition in our thinking, we are ready to create miracles for ourselves and for our world. This series has been about how to change our lives and change our worlds from the inside out — about transformation. No church, no family, no country is strong when everyone in them is weak. Transformation, the internal change of individuals, is our only hope for better lives and a better world. We've tried everything else!

In these homilies I have described this internal process. When we turn within to find the amazing spiritual powers of the mind, heart and body, we find out that God is not "out there" somewhere. He is right here, now! He is that presence "within which we live and move and have our being." (Acts 17:28) It is from within, where God lives, that we are called to transformation. I believe this is what Jesus called *metanoia,* a spiritual heart transplant!

Let's review this process of transformation. First there is the entry event, that event which I describe as the "rock that comes crashing through the windows of our lives" inviting us to change and grow. This entry event can be the death of a cherished person, a divorce, a job change, a new acquaintance, hitting bottom in an addiction, or a new book. It can be either painful or pleasant. The event can be forced on us, circumstantial, or self-initiated. The only thing that matters here is our reaction to that event! If we embrace the experience of change, we enter a transformation process. If we resist, we join the masses who choose not to grow for the sake of safety and comfort, those who commit spiritual and personal suicide. But once committed to the process of transformation, we must undergo a painful breakdown. With patient endurance, this breakdown is followed by a breakthrough. Finally, we enter the "promised land." We become that new person, we find ourselves living the new life we used to dream about!

Those who have survived the transformation process a few times no longer need to rely on the reported religious experiences of others, for they know for themselves that it works. They are ready to apply it to many areas of their lives. Once they have become convinced of its effectiveness and master its process, they are ready to become creators of their lives.

Maybe these spiritually maturing people got their first taste of transformation by embracing something that happened to them, but they have become ready to induce their own labor pains of growth. Instead of waiting for entry opportunities to happen to them, they are ready to "throw rocks through their own windows." When they reach this point, they are able to act boldly on their own behalf. They realize they can help themselves be happy. Believing in their own God-given power and strength, they can make up their minds to begin a hero's journey of transformation. Believing in their own God-given power and strength, they know that the courage to face loss, transition, rejection will be there as they break down the boundaries around who they are, what they can do, and what is possible. They look outside at the stars one night and realize that there is another world within them that is just as vast, an inner world that one can explore!

Some in our community who still believe that people are changed through conformation or reformation have always hated the fact that we will "take anybody" here at the Cathedral. They want to hear more condemnation of behaviors, more about laws, more about obedience to authority from this pulpit. I choose to preach Jesus' "conversion through invitation" method. I believe that the world can only be changed from the inside out. I have sought to share what I have discovered with you — the power of spiritual and personal transformation. I prefer being a guide to being a judge. Transformation cannot be imposed on those who are not ready, but it can be made available to those who are hungry for it. I will not be discouraged that this series of homilies has not changed the world. I am excited by the fact that some of these seeds have already sprouted in some of you. Positive reports are already coming in. I realize that I have no control over the outcome. That's between you and God! My job is merely to plant seeds!

March 21, 1993

Spirituality Is About . . .
Part 1: Spirituality is About Listening to the Voice of God

Jesus, full of the Holy Spirit, returned from the Jordan and was led by the Spirit into the desert for forty days, where he was tempted by the devil.

LUKE 4

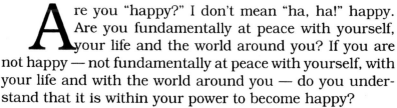

Are you "happy?" I don't mean "ha, ha!" happy. Are you fundamentally at peace with yourself, your life and the world around you? If you are not happy — not fundamentally at peace with yourself, with your life and with the world around you — do you understand that it is within your power to become happy?

Children are taught that happiness is something that comes to them through magic potions and magic spells. "Poof! Now you're happy!" Many adults go through life believing that happiness is a matter of luck. "I'd be happy if only I could be lucky enough to meet the right partner — lucky enough to find a job that paid a lot of money — lucky enough to be born into a better family — lucky enough to win the lottery." "I'd be happy if only I hadn't been so unlucky as to get cancer — if my parents hadn't died — if I hadn't married the wrong person."

Happiness is not something bestowed on us from the outside; it is something we generate from within. What happens out there may cause us aggravation and pain, but happiness is about deciding how to respond to what happens out there. Happiness is gained, not by luck or magic potions or material accumulation, but by training ourselves to look at all the good and bad in every given moment, and then choosing to focus on the good.

The ability to see clearly and choose wisely requires deliberate personal effort, courage, resourcefulness and faith! Spirituality is about developing that ability and nurturing that faith. To develop such self-mastery requires going within ourselves and finding that peaceful center which no storm can shake, then living out of that center, no matter what happens. It is in that place in our hearts that God speaks to us, and leads us to happiness regardless of circumstances. Spirituality is about developing the ability to move to that place in your heart, while tuning out all the other voices. The tragic thing about organized religion is that some people go to church all their lives and never learn this skill, never learn the spiritual techniques to make themselves happy. Those who do not learn the way to go within and find peace are out there roaming and rummaging in the physical world, running up and down one dead-end road after another, seeking the solution that isn't even out there.

Before beginning his public ministry, Jesus withdrew to a desert to sort out all the voices in his head. As a human being, he was influenced by all the theories of his day about how to be happy and fulfilled. Jesus wanted to listen to God's voice, but which voice **was** God's voice? That is why he withdrew from ordinary activity. That is why he took the time and found the space to think. The "devil" represents all those other competing voices in his head. Why not be a super social worker and feed the world by changing rocks into bread? God knows the world could use more bread!

Why not become a super king and become the ruler of the whole world? God knows you'd be a wonderful king! Why not be a super stuntman and impress millions? God knows it would be an effective way to bring more people to God! Jesus argued all these things in his mind, not just this once, but throughout his life. "When the devil had finished all this tempting, he left him to await another opportunity." (Matthew 4:13)

The feature common to all these "temptations" is that each proposes an external solution. These tempting solutions all propose to change things by changing circumstances, by manipulating things outside the human heart. Jesus rejected all such external solutions. When he came out of the desert, Jesus had his answer. He had God's direction — change your heart, change the way you think and you will experience a new world!

If you are like most people, there are hundreds of voices around you and within your own head offering suggestions about what to do, how to act, where to go and how to get there. There is only one voice worth listening to — the one whispering in your heart. If you are like me, on many days this inner voice may be drowned out by louder and shriller voices from outside. The challenge of Lent is to go into the desert, choosing a more simple life mode, so you can put your ear against your own heart and listen. That inner voice will lead you to happiness because it is God's voice. As the prophet Isaiah says in one of my favorite Scripture passages: "While from behind, a voice shall sound in your ears: 'This is the way; walk in it,' when you would turn to the right or to the left." (Isaiah 30:21)

Most of us, when we find ourselves unhappy, tend to look for the reasons around ourselves, rather than within ourselves. "He said." "She said." "He didn't." "She didn't."

"If it weren't for this." "If it weren't for that." Those demon voices try to get us to believe that happiness is out there and is being withheld from us by sinister circumstances. When we fall for these lines, we tend to settle for symbols of happiness, for emotional painkillers or jolts of pleasure. We end up believing that if we just keep these things in ready supply, we will be happy. Instead, the truth is that we can have a new world simply by changing our attitudes toward the one we have. That is the answer Jesus chose before he emerged from the desert! He called it *metanoia*, a radical personal conversion.

My friends, most of our "unhappiness" can be traced back to some very negative and lazy thinking, not to bad luck or adverse circumstances. We have the power and the responsibility to make ourselves happy. We can dramatically alter our situations by altering our thinking. Spirituality is about developing that inner discipline necessary to control our thinking. Many may genuinely want to change their thinking, but feel they do not have the spiritual discipline to do it. They haven't developed that discipline yet, maybe, because they have not yet been converted from focusing "out there." In the language of today's gospel, the devil keeps tempting us to look "out there," while Jesus tells us to "look within" and listen to God for our happiness. Lent is the time to sort out all those noisy voices in our heads, and to tune out all but that still, quiet one. Against all odds, this voice speaks to us of beauty, of human warmth and kindness, of goodness and greatness, of heroism — and it speaks to us of happiness.

March 5, 1995

Spirituality Is About . . .
Part 2: Spirituality is About Growing as a Human Being

...leave it another year while I hoe around it and manure it; then perhaps it will bear fruit. If not, it shall be cut down.

LUKE 13

———— ♥ ————

This parable is especially meaningful to me. My heart goes out to that tree because I have been that tree.

You see, I narrowly escaped being "cut down" or kicked out of the seminary soon after I enrolled. I was having a hard time on several fronts. I was not "bearing fruit" according to the school authorities. The rector called me into his office and told me to my face that I was a "hopeless case" and that he was sending me home in the morning. "Cut it down. Why should it clutter up the ground?" I fell to my knees and cried, literally, for another chance. "Sir, leave it for another year while I hoe around it and manure it; then perhaps it will bear fruit. If not, it shall be cut down."

I woke up that day and decided that I had to take charge of my life. That experience provided me with a jump-start into a process of personal and spiritual self-cultivation that has continued ever since! If I hadn't made a move, I would certainly not be here today! I believe that I was given a second chance that day. I believe, in fact, that all of us have many chances before our last chance. I find this parable autobiographic!

Originally, of course, this parable was directed toward Israel. Israel was privileged, like a fig tree growing in a vineyard. Israel had the covenant, the prophets and the commission to make God's way known on earth. But like a barren fig tree, it was not producing fruit — had not accepted the responsibility that went with its privileged position. Israel had fallen in love with money and power. This parable speaks of God's patience in spite of Israel's delayed obedience. But it also reminded the people of Israel that there will be a last chance.

But this parable is about you as well. Your life is that tree. You, working with God, are the gardener. Spirituality is about molding and shaping your own life instead of passively accepting what happens to you. Spirituality is about digging around in your own heart and soul, about attending to your own health and happiness. Spirituality is about caring for yourself enough to rattle your own cage once in a while, about committing yourself to take a good look at what is going on in your life. Spirituality is about preparing sumptuous meals to nourish your own heart and soul. Spirituality is about growing yourself as a human being. Spirituality is about working with God to produce "ongoing fruit" in our lives. God has invested so much in us. God expects results.

God expects us to realize how much he loves us, and to act on that realization by deciding to live a life that has been radically changed by our experience of that ongoing, unconditional love. God expects us to become increasingly happy people. The spiritual life is about "knocking, seeking, asking" (hoeing and fertilizing, if you wish) until we

90

bear fruit. Spirituality is not so much about preparing for death, as it is about learning to live by caring for one's own life.

This parable is about you. Is your life producing fruit? Are you growing as a human being? Do you understand that it is your responsibility to do so? You can decide to enter the world of deliberate spiritual growth by one of two roads, either something can happen **to** you or you can **choose** to change, to make something happen to you. This moment of grace can be either painful or pleasant. These entry points are moments when God snaps her fingers to get our attention. God invites us to set out and see where the path leads.

Upon setting out, we will experience an initial euphoria, followed by a series of tests during which the spiritual person must choose between dropping out in frustration, or trusting God's love and choosing to keep on walking the spiritual path. If you keep walking, slaying dragons all along the way, you will reach a higher level of happiness. But you won't be celebrating your new life too long before you will get yet another invitation to set out all over again. Not too long after you reach a new destination, you will get yet another and another and another invitation to set out once again. We can produce as much fruit in our lives as we want, depending on how much courage we have to "dig around and fertilize" our own lives.

My friends, we are challenged today to "do something with our lives." The young are challenged to understand that failure to become your own spiritual director will result in a little pleasure now and a whole lot of unhappiness later. If you want to be happy in life, you must learn to do hard things for your own good. The better you become at it — the more committed you are to the process — the happier you will be. Those of you who are middle-aged or older need to understand that just because you have never done this for yourself before does not mean that it's too late to begin. We are given many, many chances to do something with our lives. Just grab the next chance and then the next and then the next. In the spiritual world, you **can** teach an old dog new tricks. The only place we ever really get in a rut is in our own minds.

You can change your world by changing the way you look at your world. You are probably more in a heaven right now than you think! The happiest part of your life could be the part just ahead of you, if you want it to be! There is a world of difference between wishing for fruit and "digging around and fertilizing" so as to bear and have fruit! It's still not too late to become your own personal trainer in your own spiritual and personal growth program. If you have ever been told that you are a "hopeless case," you have been lied to! As long as you are alive, you have another chance. What are you waiting for?

March 19, 1995

Spirituality Is About . . .
Part 3: Spirituality is About Identifying with the Pain of Others

Let the one among you who has no sin be the first to cast a stone at her.

JOHN 8

———— ♥ ————

Whatis it with religious zealots and their distorted interest in other peoples' sex lives? Of all the possible sins in the world they might get twisted out of shape about, why is it that other peoples' sexual activity is always at the top of their lists? These zealots always claim the highest moral motives, of course! The Pharisees in John's gospel, their hands full of rocks they are ready to hurl, are almost salivating for this poor woman's blood. The Puritans of New England humiliated similar women by making them wear a scarlet letter in public. These days, here in Louisville, a doctor and his cronies are almost rabid over gay peoples' sex lives, spewing misinformation and stereotyping a whole gamut of people.

Every time some of these militants rear their heads, I remember the first such frenzied crusade I ever witnessed. It took place while I was a young priest working in the home missions in the southern part of our diocese. A local minister ranted and raved for months about sexual misconduct in our society. He went so far as to have women bring in their pant suits and families their television sets, burning them in a huge bonfire on the church's front lawn. Some months later the local newspaper reported that he had run off with the church's teenaged organist! To paraphrase Shakespeare, "the gentleman doth protest too much, me thinks!" As Jesus knew, the self-righteous and distorted outrage of some religious fanatics often says more about them than about those against whom they crusade!

The names may change, but Pharisees are always with us. These kinds of people existed in the early church as well. Apparently the story of the sinful woman we heard today was omitted from some early manuscripts of Luke's gospel, even though the story was part of a more ancient oral tradition. Apparently there were some pious fanatics who were embarrassed by Jesus' lenient response to this woman, embarrassed enough to drop this story from the text! Jesus sent the sinner away with forgiveness, despite the fact that she did not say she was sorry or promise she would never do it again! The opponents of including this story apparently thought: "My God! This kind of behavior on Jesus' part might encourage others to commit adultery. Jesus obviously made a mistake. This story must be eliminated!" Even in primitive Christianity, there were already some who were trying to remake God into the stern judge they thought he ought to be. The problem these types always have with the real Jesus is that the God he preached loves too much! He wasn't harsh enough on sinners to suit them. Yes, Jesus told the sinful woman to "avoid this sin from now on," but I suppose it is possible he may have had to forgive her "seventy times seven times" before it was over.

No wonder this story was almost left out. There is enough stuff here to give "Puritan sex patrols" a heart attack!

Notice, first of all, to whom Jesus addresses his comments in this story. Just as the parable of the "prodigal son" that we read last week was not addressed to sinners, but to the scribes and Pharisees who were complaining about the company Jesus kept — common sinners — so Jesus' focus in today's story is not on the woman alone, but is equally divided between the scribes and Pharisees, and the woman. The most shocking thing of all about this story is that by so focusing his attention, Jesus treats the woman as the social and human **equal** of the scribes and Pharisees! Jesus speaks to both about sin, the sin of sinners and the sin of those who feel the uncontrollable need to humiliate and punish sinners. Like the father's treatment of both sons in the parable we heard last week, Jesus offers grace and mercy to both the woman and her accusers.

And just what did Jesus write in the dirt with his finger that made the crowd of men armed with stones disperse in embarrassment? One of the most interesting theories about this question revolves around the Greek word translated as "to write" in the phrase "to write on the ground." This Greek word for "write" can more accurately be translated as "to write a list of things against someone." Jesus may just have bent over and written a list of the sins of the scribes and Pharisees in the dirt. When they persisted in demanding an answer from him, Jesus stood up and said to them, "Let the one among you who has no sin be the first to cast a stone." Here, too, the Greek word translated as "without sin" is interesting. This word means not just "without sin," but "without a sinful desire." Jesus is saying to them: "Yes, you may stone her — but only if you have never wanted to do the same thing yourselves." There was a silence — and then slowly the accusers drifted away, beginning with the oldest old codger all the way to the youngest cleric! Many so-called "religious" people have come up with the notion that their job in this life is to comb the world looking for sinners to condemn and punish. Somehow, it makes them feel morally superior and spiritually smug. It is their favorite short-cut to feeling holy. They believe if they can identify a few sinners and bash them, they will feel religious! But as Jesus understood and taught in today's gospel, the bashing says more about those who bash than those who are bashed!

The message for us today is simply this — we are all sinners. Each of us needs to focus on our own sins and resist the temptation to judge others. If Jesus could treat a scarlet woman and her religious accusers as social and human equals, why can't we? Why do we need to dig holes for other people? I don't know about you, but I have never actually motivated another human being to change by any of my condemning and judging behavior. On the other hand, I have stacks and stacks of letters from people who were motivated to change their lives because of the accepting message Jesus taught which has poured out of this pulpit over the last twelve years. The word compassion means "to suffer with." To be compassionate means that we realize that, whatever someone else is dealing with, "there but for the grace of God go I." To be compassionate means identifying with the pain of others. Spirituality is about being compassionate. Spirituality is about the inner struggle to reach that place in our hearts where we realize the "there is part of everybody in me."

April 2, 1995

96

Discipleship
Part 1: Hospitality

He who welcomes you welcomes me, and he who welcomes me welcomes him who sent me.

MATTHEW 10

——— ♥ ———

One of the first priests to work in frontier Kentucky was a Frenchman by the name of Anthony Salmon. Father Salmon came to Kentucky in February, 1799 and died in November of that same year. Around the first of October 1799, Father Salmon caught a violent cold which confined him to bed for six weeks at his Nerinckx, Kentucky cabin. He didn't have time for a cold. He was determined to travel to a farm sixteen miles away, almost to nearby Bardstown, where he had an appointment to meet with a lady whom he was instructing in preparation for her baptism.

Father Salmon was a poor horseman and, though he was feeble from his recent illness, no one could dissuade him from making the trip. It was the ninth day of November and snow covered the rugged and difficult road. About a mile outside Bardstown he was thrown violently from his horse, flung against a tree, leaving him mortally wounded in the chest and head. He dragged himself to the side of the road and sat against a tree from noon until evening. One young boy out cutting wood discovered Father Salmon, but the boy's bigoted, anti-Catholic employer would not allow him to summon aid, saying, "He's only a priest and he's probably drunk." When help did arrive some twelve hours later, Father Salmon was taken to a farm near the present-day Motherhouse of the Sisters of Charity of Nazareth. He died there the next evening. His was the first funeral for a priest in Kentucky, and his death reduced the number of priests working in Kentucky to a grand total of two!

Today, I don't want to talk about hostility, but its opposite — hospitality. This homily is part of a series on discipleship, that discipline of trying to become Christ-like. Like our Master who welcomed everyone, even "welcoming sinners and eating with them," (Luke 15:2) we are called to welcome each other, without exception. Hospitality is not an option. It is fundamental to discipleship.

But before you start thinking about sweet kindness, polite tea parties, and inviting those strange neighbors over for cocktails, let me say that the biblical concept of "hospitality" has a lot more depth than that! In our culture, "hospitality" has lost much of its power because it has become a weak synonym for "being nice to people you like." What we're talking about here is much more serious than that, much more! Let me give you a little background.

Our forefathers and foremothers in the faith were nomadic people. For hundreds and hundreds of years, they had been people of the desert. In the desert, hospitality is not a nicety; it is an absolute necessity. One would die without it. Several unwritten laws governing the act of hospitality developed over centuries of experience. This harsh reality of desert life lead to the belief that anyone was entitled to hospitality from any host — friend or enemy. The guest, once received, was considered sacred. The host had a solemn and sacred duty to protect his guest from any and all harm even if it cost the life of a family member! In exchange, the guest was bound to commit no offense against anyone which would bring pain or embarrassment to the host. The guest was expected to stay from one to three days, depending on local custom. No charge was made and no payment was accepted. This seriousness about hospitality grew out of an absolute necessity for survival, not some weak idea about being nice to people!

These principles or unwritten laws about hospitality slowly became an important part of Israel's religion. The guest, the traveler, the visitor, the stranger reminded the people of Israel of the time they were strangers and were treated harshly as slaves in Egypt. The guest, the traveler, the visitor, the stranger reminded the people of Israel of its present condition as temporary guests on this earth. It was a simple theology. Ancient Israel believed that guests, the traveler, the visitor, the stranger needed to be loved in the name of the God who first loved God's people. It was a simple theology. Ancient Israel believed that the guest, the traveler, the visitor, and the stranger bore precious "blessings" from God. The exchange between host and guest enriched the lives of both. It was a theology that grew out of centuries of experiencing the necessity to be one's "brother's or sister's keeper" in an often inhospitable landscape.

Jesus came from that tradition, lived it perfectly, and taught his disciples, both then and now, to do the same — to welcome strangers, sinners, children, the hurting, the sick, foreigners, travelers and prophets. He told them, "When you welcome one of these, you welcome me." Jesus promised his followers, then and now, that even the simplest hospitable practical gesture will be rewarded and reminds us there is a blessing from God in every welcome.

For today's disciples, people who are actively trying to become Christ-like, the requirement to offer hospitality is no less negotiable. In fact, hospitality may be even more important today when hostility toward others seems to escalate daily. But before you rush out and move a street person into your spare bedroom, pick up a backseat full of hitchhikers or host a series of backyard barbecues for the whole neighborhood, let me remind you that the spiritual practice of hospitality needs to be adapted to today's realities. The term "hospitality" need not be limited to its literal sense of receiving strangers, but needs to be understood to require a fundamentally loving attitude toward our fellow human beings which can be expressed in a variety of ways.

Biblical hospitality is first and fundamentally about having a loving and compassionate attitude toward all people, no matter who they are, friend and enemy alike. Out of such a hospitable mind will inevitably come hospitable behaviors and actions. As Jesus said " . . . every good tree bears good fruit." (Matthew 7:17) Here are just a few examples of how we practice biblical hospitality as modern-day disciples. When we, as a parish, welcome all kinds of people as parishioners and guests, we are practicing biblical hospitality. When we reach out to embrace the whole community, seeking respectful dialogue with all religions through our Cathedral Heritage Foundation programs and welcoming people of all beliefs to community celebrations in the Cathedral, we are practicing biblical hospitality. When we support the work of ministry to our street people we extend potentially life-saving hospitality to those in the harsh urban landscape.

When we, as individuals, commit ourselves to community building projects, whether sponsored by this parish or by other groups, we are practicing biblical hospitality. These are programs that work with kids, the elderly, the mentally handicapped, immigrants or programs that work to eliminate racism, sexism, ageism, homophobia and injustices of any kind, and our participation places us where we can experience God's unexpected blessings. Parents practice biblical hospitality when they courageously welcome children and raise them with love and patience, often sacrificing many of their own needs and wants, thus loving their children as God has loved them. Marriage partners practice biblical hospitality when they treasure their partners as bearers of blessings from God and find their holiness in simply being a source of life and strength for them, day in and day out.

Biblical hospitality is a serious duty for serious disciples and God knows how desperately the world needs its restoration. Biblical hospitality begins in the mind and heart. It begins with an attitude of reverence and care for all of God's people no matter what condition they are in. We can practice this spiritual discipline without approving of, engaging in or even knowing about everything other people do or believe. Jesus, in fact, taught us to love, to welcome all people into our hearts, even our enemies. All people are potentially messengers from God bearing blessings that will be revealed in the human exchange of welcoming and being welcomed. Ask anyone who is seriously engaged in this rewarding spiritual discipline: I can tell you I have always gotten back more than I have given, just as Jesus promised.

I have always wondered what Father Salmon might have accomplished if he had been offered hospitality and survived. I wonder what blessings the bigot and the priest might have brought into each other's lives, if the bigot had chosen a different response. I always wonder how many blessings I have denied myself because of fear, by being hostile rather than hospitable to some of the people who have crossed my path over the years. I challenge you to wonder about the blessings you may have missed in your life. Discipleship calls for us to welcome all as we have been welcomed — to practice the virtue of biblical hospitality confident that we will be blessed.

June 30, 1996

Discipleship
Part 2: The Payoffs of Pain And The Satisfactions of Discipleship

Your souls will find rest, for my yoke is easy and my burden light.

MATTHEW 11

——— ❤ ———

Every once in a while I like to sit on my front porch, smoke a cheap cigar, and watch the world go by. On Eastern Parkway, at least, it does seem that on any given day the whole world goes by. I find it so relaxing to watch all kinds of bizarre stuff going on without feeling one bit responsible for doing anything about it! Joggers are an interesting lot. Every few minutes, you see some sweaty, overweight person, puffing his or her way down the sidewalk. You can tell it's the beginning of a well-intentioned, but short-lived, resolution to lose weight and get into shape. You realize they mean well, but discipline is lacking. You see them once, maybe twice, but they seldom last. My heart goes out to them. Then there are the regulars: the day in and day out, rain or shine, types. They proudly strut their stuff and rightly so. They are tanned and lean, with not one ounce of fat to be seen anywhere on their firm little bodies. They enjoy showing off the results of years of self-discipline. Don't you just hate them?

Seriously, though, have you ever noticed that there are always two sides to every discipline? There's pain and gain.

Those joggers did not achieve their lean frames by giving in to every lazy whim and addiction that comes along. They paid for those bodies with years of sweat, abstinence and resolve.

Discipline is about embracing short-term pain for the sake of long-term gain. Blessed are the children who are taught discipline early. Blessed are the adults who can practice self-discipline successfully. One of the tragedies of our time may be that our comfort-seeking and pleasure-addicted culture is forgetting the pay-offs of pain.

The word "discipleship" comes from the word "discipline." A disciple is one who freely embraces discipline. A disciple realizes the payoffs of pain. Jesus describes his discipline, what he calls his "yoke," as "refreshing," "restful," "easy" and "light." The word "easy" is an unfortunate translation, however. The Greek word *crestos*, translated here as "easy," really means "tailor-made" or "well-fitting." It's a word from the carpenter shop of Jesus' youth. In Palestine, ox-yokes were made of wood. The ox was brought in, the measurements were made, the yoke was roughed out and the ox was brought back in for an adjustment. The rough hewn yoke was carefully whittled and whittled until it was *crestos*, until it fit perfectly and did not gall the neck. The yoke was tailor-made to fit the ox.

"My yoke, my discipline, is also *crestos*" Jesus tells his disciples. My yoke is a joy to carry because it is well-suited. Jesus was comparing his spiritual discipline to that of the religion of his day. The Jewish religion of his day had evolved to a point where it was overly complicated, with endless lists of rules, regulations and sanctions. The Jewish Law was often referred to as a "yoke." For the orthodox Jew, religion had become a burden. Jesus said of the Scribes and Pharisees, "They bind heavy burdens, hard to bear,

104

and lay them on people's shoulders." (Matthew 23:4) Jesus tells his disciples that his brand of religion, not a new religion, but a renewed religion, brings refreshment, rest and lightness, not guilt, dread, aggravation and frustration.

Jesus lifted the burden of a legalistic religion from the backs of his disciples. Paul is the most famous case. That's what Paul's conversion was all about. Paul was freed from a slavish relation to legalisms and given a joy-filled relation to God. Jesus once said to his disciples, "I do not call you slaves, . . . I call you friends." (John 15:15)

Remember, this was God talking to human beings through the mouth of Jesus. God's word came from the mouth of Jesus. Jesus wanted to give his followers a life-giving religion that is released through discipleship, not an easy religion in our sense of that word. Like the payoffs of regular exercise, the satisfaction of keeping one's commitments or the contentment of a deep and long-lasting relationship, becoming like Jesus does not happen without discipline. A disciple must give deliberate, focused and consistent attention to the life-giving path that Jesus walked.

Religion is becoming wearisome for some people today. It has all gotten too complicated. Some are mired down in secondary issues. Some advocate a religion which has recently become over-identified with a right wing political agenda, as if that were the only way to be a disciple. Certainly, we don't need some kind of overly polite religion with no guts, but just as certainly we do not need another round of the Crusades and the Inquisitions! Why does it always have to be a choice between two extremes? Why not a challenging religion with heart? Why not a religion that gives life, rather than draining the life out of you?

We can have that kind of religion — one that demands our best and challenges us out of our resistance to grow. I have spent my entire priesthood looking under the obvious problems of the church and trying to find that refreshing religion that Jesus talked about. If I hadn't found a corner of it, I would not be here today. For the last thirteen years, I have tried to preach that kind of discipleship from this pulpit.

My friends, you are disciples. Take charge of your spiritual quest. Get into your discipleship. Take the life-giving and refreshing yoke of Jesus on your shoulders. You don't have to wait until some institutional change is made. You can be a disciple where you are, right here in a struggling Catholic Church in this day and time. You can look at the wisdom in both the right and the left and ignore the lunatic fringe on both sides. You can do it now. You can begin here. Decide to give what's left of this Mass your deliberate, focused attention. That is one of the most important disciplines of discipleship, not just attending a Mass, but celebrating Eucharist!

July 7, 1996

Discipleship
Part 3: The Work of Discipleship —
Receiving and Sowing Seeds

Some seeds fell on the footpath. Some fell on rocky ground.
Some fell among thorns. But some seeds fell on good soil
and produced a crop.

MATTHEW 13

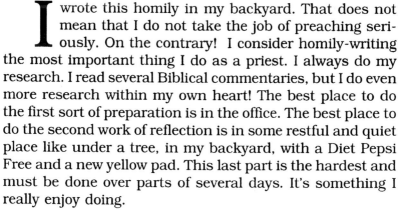

I wrote this homily in my backyard. That does not mean that I do not take the job of preaching seriously. On the contrary! I consider homily-writing the most important thing I do as a priest. I always do my research. I read several Biblical commentaries, but I do even more research within my own heart! The best place to do the first sort of preparation is in the office. The best place to do the second work of reflection is in some restful and quiet place like under a tree, in my backyard, with a Diet Pepsi Free and a new yellow pad. This last part is the hardest and must be done over parts of several days. It's something I really enjoy doing.

As usual this week I did my reading of scriptural commentaries on today's gospel, but then I could go no further. All I could come up with was a dull list of first century Palestinian agricultural practices. As hard as I tried, I could not make it interesting even to myself, much less to you. I decided to forget about explaining to you the intricacies of what the parable says. I'll simply cut to the chase and tell you what it means to me personally by sharing my backyard reflections on key phrases with you. Hopefully, you and I have enough in common that you will be able to see yourself in these reflections. Instead of us trying to identify what people are which kind of soil in this parable, let's assume that we, ourselves, are all four kinds of soil at the same time.

"The sower went out to sow good seed." This phrase from today's parable tells me that God is always busy, never letting up. God is constantly sowing the seeds of divine truth and good ideas in our hearts, hoping that we will be open and receptive to his seeds. I know this to be true in my life, certainly. I came to believe, a few years back, that the intolerant and aggravated God that I grew up on just does not exist. I know now that image was a distortion, like an image in a carnival hall of mirrors. Since then, I have come to believe that our God loves us without condition. God's love is an aggressive love. God's out working hard to win us over and to bless us. I have no problem whatsoever believing what Jesus is saying in this parable, that God is always sowing good seeds in our hearts, always throwing the possibility of new life at us, always hoping He will get a good reception.

"Some of God's good seed fell on the footpath." Sometimes I just want God to leave me alone. I don't want to be bothered. I don't want God messing in my life and asking me to change, to do this or that or to improve in any way. I may not like the status quo, but I also don't want to do all that work required to change things. I just want to do what I want to do and be left alone. When that happens, my head and my heart harden like the packed down dirt on a well-worn path, and God's seeds bounce off me like water off a duck's back. I just won't let those seeds in and so they have no chance of sprouting, much less taking root or growing to maturity. I can stay in that frame of mind for a few hours, a few days or even a few years.

"Some of God's good seed fell on shallow ground." Sometimes I get excited about some religious idea, but sometimes I never get beyond the good idea stage. It's sort of like one of those national polls on prayer and church attendance. While ninety-five percent of the population may think it is a great idea, a very small percentage actually pray and attend church. I keep telling myself that I could handle stress if I would do more regular meditation, but I can't seem to get around to it. The seed may have sprouted, it may be a great idea, but it is left to dry out and starve to death. Like seeds in shallow ground, making resolutions without follow-through is like planting a garden and then forgetting about it. God only knows how many of God's seeds I have taken in and then let die! And I don't believe God holds that against me. These were just missed opportunities for me!

"Some of God's good seed fell among thorns." Sometimes my heart is divided in its loyalties. I want to be good and rotten at the same time. Instead of appreciating my life as a priest, the grass sometimes looks greener on the other side of the fence. Sometimes my mind drifts away from how blessed I am to what's missing in my life and I let that pull me down. It's similar to being married and having a roaming eye. When that happens, the resources I need to be a good priest and happy person are wasted to feed "thorns." When that happens, my heart divides and I end up doing things without having my heart fully in them. Then, my effectiveness is seriously diminished.

"Some of God's good seed falls on rich and receptive soil." Sometimes the seed falls on good soil! I'm not all bad! Sometimes I am open and receptive and I do nurture some

109

of the good seeds that God sows in me! I did this at age thirteen, when I got into my dad's car and asked him to take me to the seminary. Most of the people I knew predicted that I would not make it and they told me so. I nurtured a good seed when I was thirty-nine years old, the day I accepted Archbishop Kelly's invitation to become pastor of the Cathedral. I almost said "No." I did it again the day I decided to be reconciled with my dad when I was age thirty-seven. I almost backed out twice. I've nurtured good seed several times in my life and, like the harvest in the parable, the good results continue to come. God forgives me when I fail, is proud of me when I succeed and loves me in either case. In the meanwhile, He continues to sow His seeds.

The work of the disciple is two-fold, however. We are called to be receptive to God's seeds in our own hearts, and we are called to sow the seeds of God in the hearts of others.

As a priest, I share this work especially with parents, teachers, social workers or anyone else who works to make a difference in other people's lives. We should not be afraid of our lack of results. It is true that some of what we sow will fall on deaf hearts. Some of what we sow will be short-lived. Some of what we sow will be compromised by other voices and will never reach its full potential. But the fabulous news is that some of what we sow will bear abundant fruit. We need to remember that we have no control over the kind of soil on which the seed we sow will fall. That's between the other person and God. Our job is to keep on sowing as freely as we can, knowing that, yes, some of what we sow will indeed land on good soil and produce abundantly.

July 14, 1996

110

Discipleship
Part 4: The Passion of Discipleship

In his joy, he goes and sells all that he has and buys that field....he went out and sold all that he had and bought that one pearl.

MATTHEW 13

———— ♥ ————

Nothing is quite as exciting as the idea of finding a buried treasure. I remember one incident from my own childhood when I stumbled onto such a hidden treasure. I was about ten years old. My brother and I were playing in the woods that my father owned, behind our parish church.

This was back before garbage trucks came to the country. In those days, everybody, including the parish staff, threw their junk into old sink holes. One day as my brother and I were playing, we decided to check out the latest deposits in the nearby sink hole. Our exploration turned up one of those old votive candle stands into which you drop coins before lighting a candle. The thing was so old and dilapidated that the pastor had thrown it out. I had a stick in my hands, and I decided for some reason to give the coin box a big whack. All of a sudden, it started spitting out coins in a stream like I had never seen in my whole life. That stand had been so packed with coins that it didn't even rattle or else our pastor would surely have emptied it before he threw it away. When the stream ended, there were more coins on the ground than this little country boy had ever seen in one place! Once we quit jumping up and down, my brother and I bagged up the loot and stashed it in a secret hiding place, while we worked through whether to keep our mouths shut or turn the windfall in to the pastor. It was the biggest moral dilemma of my childhood. I'll tell you what we did at the end of this homily.

Treasure tales are common in the literature of almost every culture. The ancient world loved treasure tales. We have two such stories in our gospel reading today. (Matthew 13:44-52) Finding a buried treasure was always possible back then, because burying one's valuables was the best protection against thieves. Often, people died without anyone knowing where they had buried their money and jewels. A farm could be bought and sold several times without anyone ever discovering the hidden stash. By law, whoever owned the field, owned the treasure. Likewise, in the ancient world people placed great value on pearls. The wealthy sought them out and wore them in necklaces. Common folk tended to venerate them to the point of superstition. One folk belief, that whoever owned a pearl would always be happy, was widely shared.

So Jesus began to speak of hidden treasures and exquisite pearls, intensely engaging the imagination of his listeners. Jesus used the images of a man who stumbles on a buried treasure and the merchant who finds a most exquisite pearl as ways to teach simple people about what it's like to discover a precious and valuable inner reality. A parable helps people move from something they know in the physical world to something they do not know in the spiritual world.

What is that treasure so valuable that a person should go to any lengths to possess it? Jesus was not really talking about finding silver or gold or jewels. He is talking about finding a precious reality within ourselves, about finding the Kingdom of God, the Divine Presence within. In reality, the heart searches not for gold or jewels or even the big lottery payoff, but for spiritual realities. Most of us assume that those material things will give us what our heart seeks. But, "Our hearts are restless, till they rest in thee," St. Augustine reminds us.

In these treasure stories both the landowner and the merchant, having found their treasure, are willing "in their joy" to sell everything they have to possess it. It's the same enthusiasm the first disciples displayed when they found Jesus. They dropped everything to follow him. It's the same enthusiasm which has enabled saints and martyrs throughout history to sacrifice everything, even their earthly lives. It's the same enthusiasm St. Paul had when he wrote, "I count all things rubbish compared to gaining Christ." (Phil 3:8) The Kingdom of God, Jesus says, is a treasure so valuable that, once found, a person will gladly and enthusiastically give up everything to possess it.

Something is wrong here. If all this is true — if we are supposed to respond to the Kingdom of God like a landowner who finds a buried treasure or a merchant who finds the most exquisite pearl in the whole world — then why is religion so boring and why are religious people so bored? Could it be that our teachers and preachers have not found this treasure themselves, and so are unable to present it to others in a convincing way?

Who in religion today is talking about the "hidden treasure" and the "pearl of great price?" Certainly not the noisy religious right! They are not convincing people that when they find the Kingdom of God, they will be willing to give up all else to possess it. Instead, these people are neck deep in political maneuvers and control tactics, cheap substitutes for the real thing. They believe they can demonstrate their conviction and strengthen their shaky faith by forcing conformity onto others. The fact of the matter is, once the "treasure" is discovered and the "pearl" is found, people do not need to be manipulated into conformity. They will gladly give up everything else! But neither is the liberal religious left talking about the "hidden treasure" and the "pearl of great price." They are too busy trying to come up with a formula for making changes in the structure which they assume will bring happiness and faith to all! There is no joy coming from this camp either! They are too busy being angry at the institution and countering the political antics of the religious right with their own political antics! We need an institution. We need rules. We need order. But if all those things do not flow from the hearts of people who have found the buried treasure and the valuable pearl, religious practice will be distorted. People will end up in idolatry, worshiping the external forms of religion, as a substitute for discovering the essence of religion deep in their hearts!

Whether we are first century disciples or twenty-first century disciples, Jesus tells us in this parable that three movements are essential to discipleship. We have to find the kingdom within. Once we have found it, we will gladly give up (sell) everything else to possess (buy) it. What is the "it" we need to find? What is the "it" that we will sacrifice everything we have to possess? It's the knowledge, the realization, that the divine Creator and Sustainer is with us already (within our body, mind, soul and spirit) already loving us without condition! That realization will make the value of everything else pale by comparison! It is the realization that all you have ever dreamed about is already yours and you have been walking over it, unaware, all along! Like a buried treasure, it's beautiful and it's yours and it's free and you didn't do anything to earn it!

Oh, by the way, my brother and I reluctantly turned our "treasure" back over to the pastor, and rejoiced when he gave us a generous reward!

July 28, 1996

Lest You Become Disheartened: When Ideals and Reality Meet

— ❤ —

Church Wars

Then Peter approaching asked him, "Lord, if my brother sins against me, how often must I forgive him? As many as seven times?" Jesus answered, "I say to you, not seven times but seventy times seven times.

MATTHEW 18

------- ♥ -------

One of my favorite questions for young couples who are preparing for marriage is: "What do you expect to happen in your marriage?" The usual answers are: "sharing," "communicating," and, of course, "loving." In twenty-five years, not one single couple has mentioned that they expect "fighting." I always give them a bit of advice anyway, just in case in some improbable eventuality, they should turn out to be just like every other married couple on the planet. My unsolicited advice is: "It's not a question of whether you will fight, but a question of how fairly you will fight. So you need to learn to fight fairly."

I think there must be at least as many people who believe that church people should not fight. I have no idea where people get such a stupid and unrealistic idea. More than a few people even conclude that conflict among church people is a valid reason to leave the church community. This silly belief betrays a total ignorance of Scripture and of human nature.

Jesus never gave us a commandment: "Thou shalt not fight in the church." He knew humans better than that! He did tell us, however, that each time we do fight, we must

119

forgive. He certainly wouldn't have given us that advice if he had not known we would be needing it. We are even given instructions in this gospel on how to fight fairly!

For those who are scandalized by fighting, arguing, and conflict in the church today, I have one bit of advice: Read your Bible! Even the apostles and saints did it! James and John made a move to get the best seats in heaven behind the backs of the other ten apostles. When the ten found out about it, they were "indignant." "Indignant" means a wrathful, angry or contemptuous response. Even at the Last Supper, Jesus had to intervene in an argument among them about who was "the greatest," and that wasn't the first time he had to step in. Paul and Barnabas had to quit working together because of a violent quarrel. Paul even called Peter "two-faced." Obviously, fighting was pretty common in the early church or else we wouldn't be reading about this three-point plan for resolving conflicts in the church!

This three-point plan for resolving conflicts in the church (first, a private word; then a companion to go with you; and, finally, refer it to the church) cannot be a direct quote from Jesus because the church did not yet exist. Rather, these words are the sentiments of Jesus that were applied to the actual lived experiences of the early church. The plan is a later application of Jesus' teachings to conflicts which had arisen in the church. This generally workable process has one flaw. Suppose the person doesn't listen to the one-on-one discussion of the problem and the problems cannot be resolved with the help of a witness or even the church? The plan then calls for the sinner "to be treated like a tax-collector or a Gentile." What does that mean? Three strikes and you're out? Kick him out and treat him like a hopeless outsider? What about forgiving seventy times seven times?

When Jesus spoke of "Gentiles and tax collectors," he did so with sympathy and gentleness. They were his friends. No, I imagine Jesus would have said something like this: "When you have done all this, when you have given the sinner every chance, when he/she remains stubborn and obstinate, continue to love them as I love them. Never quit trying, never give up — remember what I did for Matthew and Zaccheus. Remember I loved Judas and reached out to him up to the last minute! There is always a chance for conversion, always a chance for reform."

Conflict has always been part of the church. It's never been about avoiding conflict, but about "fighting fair." The apostles fought. The great saints fought. We still fight in the church. Father Clyde Crews, our archdiocesan historian, told me two stories about conflict in his history of this Cathedral.

Around the turn of the last century, in the days of the talented and energetic Monsignor Bouchet, communication got so bad in the rectory next door that the priests stopped speaking to each other. When the priests had to communicate, they wrote letters and mailed them — to people who lived in the same house! I found myself wondering what happened to drive them to such extreme behavior. I guess it must have been the combination of celibacy and the lack of air conditioning! Father Crews also gave me a copy of a handwritten note from 1927. Its author was a good Catholic lay person who wrote to the chancery about a priest who lived in the Cathedral rectory. "It is alleged that he associates with a low and mean class of people... with idle and lazy men who lounge in the pool rooms and stores around town and never work. He will invite them to go hunting with him, furnishing them with shells. It is said that he

121

frequents pool rooms etc... that he has been seen to play the slot machines."

I have my own small file of nasty letters of complaint about some of the things I have done or said. God only knows what they have on me at the chancery! Fighting, complaining and arguing among God's holy people seems to be as old as Cain and Abel! Even the commandments don't outlaw fighting and arguing, but just talk about fighting fairly: "thou shalt not kill" and "thou shalt not bear false witness" and "thou shalt not covet!" Even while Jesus told us to "love one another," he obviously knew we were going to fail, because he also taught us to forgive seventy times seven times, and told us that peacemakers are "blessed." A fair and respectful argument, disagreement or fight has never been a valid reason to leave the church: Never has been and never will be!

My fellow parishioners, the church is and always has been made up of ordinary human beings. As human beings, we all have our flaws and limitations. The more we get to know each other, the more we see those limitations. I have made an effort to make this place as welcoming as possible. I have tried to accept you as you are. I have tried to be the best priest I can be for you, but I am not perfect — far from it! This is a high-pressured and demanding job, especially during this renovation period. Sometimes I get irritable, distracted and have a short fuse. I try my best to apologize when I act this way. In turn, I try to accept your limitations. I hope that you will continue to do the same for me. Every church needs peacemakers. We are all called to forgive each other and to make peace within our parish family, within the various ministries and between individuals who worship here. When hurt feelings and misunderstandings do occur, the Lord wants us to work it out. We are indeed each different from each other, but this does not mean we have to be antagonistic. We can reverence the difference and work together as equals, always ready to forgive and be reconciled. There are no perfect pastors or parishioners, so we must learn to be vigilant in our relationships with each other, and generous with our forgiveness. We may not be perfect, but we can be magnanimous!

September 5, 1993

Let Go Of The Peanut

... as the number of disciples grew, the ones who spoke Greek complained that their widows were being neglected in the daily distribution of food as compared with the widows of those who spoke Hebrew.

ACTS OF THE APOSTLES 6

———— ♥ ————

Just three weeks ago, we read in this very same book of the Bible about a small church filled with sweetness and light. They even "held everything in common and divided everything according to each one's need." (Acts 4:32-35) This week, two chapters later, they are complaining about their "fair share." That first picture of the church is nice, but this last picture is more like the church I know and love!

This story is not just about "deacons," it is also about how the early church solved a problem that came with rapid growth. It's the early Christian community's version of the priest shortage. There were twelve apostles, eleven old ones and a replacement for Judas, but new members were coming in droves! "Every day, the Lord added to their number. . ." is what the book of Acts says. (Acts 2:47) The apostles could not do well all that needed to be done, so they held on to what was unique to them and gave the rest away! As a result, more believers were drawn into ministry with the apostles. A problem suddenly turned into an opportunity. Just as the complaints of Greek widows about a lack of food brought a change into the church, contemporary complaints about the lack of spiritual food from a dwindling number of priests continues to bring about changes in our church. The church that has the courage to change when needed is a living, breathing, healthy church — one is which the Holy Spirit is alive instead of merely a stuffed, mounted, dust-catching symbol on the church wall! These people were smart enough to change when it was time! God was alive in them!

As I read this story again this year this insight is what jumped out at me, precisely because we are living it! In the past ten years, this parish has gone from being served by five priests to having one full-time priest who is assisted by another priest part-time, while the congregation has grown from two hundred individuals to about two thousand. At Christmas and Easter, we pack in more and more people in every year. The reality of our growth hit me two weeks ago when I was scheduled to say a few words to our Sunday School kids on their last day of classes. I was bowled over when I went into Marian Hall. It was packed with kids!

How did the apostles solve their problem? They "let go." Their "letting go" empowered others. As the church expanded, they gave away part of their ministry to others. As the number of priests has shrunk, the number of parishioners has grown. As a result, we have had the opportunity to do the same. A lot of what priests used to do around here is now being done by lay staff members and our deacons. These people, in turn, have empowered many, many more! There are more people involved in ministry today than at any other time in the one hundred and eight-seven year history of this parish!

"Let go and let God." I find myself trying to learn that yet one more time! As much as part of me would like to hold on to parts of our recent past as we go into the future, it cannot be done. There is a process in motion here, an unfolding of a new reality that is no longer under my control. As one of you said to me a few weeks ago, "Relax! Your dream is coming true!" I have become a bundle of raw nerves recently, ever since they started tearing up the church and offices to proceed with the restoration.

It took a few days off for me to see that I was having a simple panic attack. But panic is something that comes from within a person, not something that attacks from without. Lurking behind all those raw nerves was a plain old fear of the unknown, fear of losing control and grief over the losing the familiar. It was my mind trying to hold on to the past which was creating my pain. Now that I know what I have to do, I am trying to do it. As Jesus says so eloquently in the Gospel of Mark, "Fear is useless; what is needed is trust!" (Mark 5:36) Or, to paraphrase a card I got for my birthday, "the unfolding of [this project] is not an issue of competence or control. It is an issue of faith." As I've had to remind myself, you cannot arrive at a distant shore without saying goodbye to the old one!

The apostles can teach us a lot today. New realities constantly occur in all of our lives. Sometimes they happen to us and sometimes we bring it on ourselves. These new realities often produce fear: What if it doesn't work? What if I can't handle it? What if I can't go back? What if I lose this or that? What if...?

Is it retirement? Is it a favorite way of doing things? Is it unemployment? Is it an unplanned pregnancy? Is it children leaving home? Is it an unexpected illness? Is it a massive restoration program? When we resist and fight change, we create pain for ourselves. When we "let go and let God," we gain a freedom previously unimagined. When the apostles "let go" they enjoyed the freedom to "concentrate on prayer and the ministry of the word." Then, the Word was able to spread, while at the same time the number of disciples in Jerusalem increased enormously.

I leave you with a wonderful story I heard on retreat in January. It must be an Eastern fable. It's about how they catch monkeys for zoos. The hunters fill an empty gourd with peanuts, cut a small hole in the gourd and fasten it to a tree. After dark, the monkeys come out and reach into the gourds for the peanuts. With a peanut clutched in their fists, they cannot pull their hands out. All the monkeys would have to do to free themselves is let go of the peanut. Instead, they hold on to the peanut and howl until their captors come and take them off to zoos. We humans are often like that! We hang on to things and refuse to let go of them no matter how miserable we get! All we would have to do is let go of the peanut! How many "peanuts" is your mind holding on to today? Are you squeezing them tightly, howling and feeling miserable? Is it an old grudge? An old way of doing things? A favorite addiction? A consuming resentment? The mirage of control? So many things improve when we let go of these "peanuts," whether it is a first century church member or one of us!

May 9, 1993

A Walk On Water

Peter got out of the boat and began to walk on water, moving toward Jesus. But when he perceived how strong the wind was, becoming frightened, he began to sink, and cried out, "Lord, save me!" Jesus at once stretched out his hand and caught him.

MATTHEW 14

———— ♥ ————

If Hollywood were to film a movie scene of today's gospel reading, it would, no doubt, show a small boat-load of terrified and screaming disciples, unmercifully battered by rain and wind in pitch darkness broken by intermittent lightening, the vessel's twisted and ripped sails dangling in the background. No doubt the film makers would picture Peter clumsily making his way across the water, like a staggering drunk trying to reach something solid. Jesus would, no doubt, be dressed in white, standing with hands outstretched, with light radiating from his robes and an almost condescending smile on his face.

Though this might be a standard Hollywood approach to depicting this event, it would give us absolutely no insight at all into what this story means. We need to be able to unlock the message between the lines and behind the words. As in many other great Bible stories, there is a whole lot more going on here than just another stunt in a storm!

If I were to film this story, instead of a boat-load of

terrified first century fishermen, I might show a room full of recovering alcoholics or drug addicts. They too, have answered the invitation to "come to me across the water." Their storms may be more emotional and spiritual than physical, but their fear would be just as intense, and the courage and faith needed just as important. If I were to film this story, instead of a boat-load of terrified first century fishermen, I might show an elderly widow alone in her small apartment, retirement home room or empty house. With her children gone and her husband dead, she too, is trying to answer the invitation to "come to me across the water." Her storm may be more emotional and spiritual than physical, but her fear would be just as intense, and the courage and faith needed just as important. If I were to film this story, instead of a boat-load of terrified first century fishermen, I might show a group of adolescents trying to make the transition to adulthood. They too, are answering the invitation to "come to me across the water." Their storms may be more emotional and spiritual than physical, but their fear would be just as intense and the courage and faith needed just as important. If I were to film this story, instead of a boat-load of terrified first century fishermen, I might show patients in a cancer or HIV clinic or parents with chronically ill children. They, too, are answering the call to "come to me across the water." The storms they face are emotional, physical, and spiritual, the fear would be just as intense, and the courage and faith needed just as important.

Yes, there are many ways to film this story because so many of us find ourselves in Peter's shoes, with the wind against us, taking faith-walks in spite of our fear, one shaky step at a time.

Jesus' call to Peter in the storm is one of the most beautiful stories in the New Testament. During times of great doubt, stress, loss and persecution, the earliest Christians repeated this story over and over again to give themselves courage. Generations of early Christians saw themselves in this story. When these earliest believers were being hacked to death, humiliated and tortured by a series of hostile Roman Emperors, they turned to this story. They saw themselves as that small group of disciples, huddled in a little boat, caught out on a lake after dark in a storm. To comfort each other and to give themselves strength, they remembered Peter's walk of faith. They remembered how Jesus reached out and caught him. When they finally got around to writing their stories down, they included this one so that people like us would likewise be encouraged during the storms of life.

Storms are an inevitable part of Christian life. This story demonstrates in a very vivid way the kind of faith that followers of Jesus must develop. People often get the impression that problems and set-backs in life are a sign of God's absence, signs that God doesn't care. The point of this story is that God calls Peter to faith, not on some sunshine-filled day, but in the midst of a storm! Some of us imagine that God is to be found only when things are going well. In fact, God's most insistent calls are often made in times of strife and struggle. Sometimes it is only when we have reached the end of our ropes, when we have exhausted our own strength, or when we find that we have nowhere else to turn, that we find God. It is often then that we find him and love him even more dearly. Conquered fear always brings forth new courage and strengthened faith. Ask anybody who has survived a tragedy with their faith intact!

Many of you reading these words are being called to take a faith-walk to "come to me across the waters." You are facing cancer, AIDS, unemployment, depression, a handicap, retirement, old age, chronic illness, loneliness, loss of loved ones, guilt, public humiliation, divorce or an unplanned pregnancy. Maybe you are struggling with your sexual orientation. Maybe you are an unwed mother. Maybe you are a homesick teenager away from home for the first time. Maybe you have almost given up ever finding a suitable partner. Maybe you are waiting to hear the results of a biopsy or other medical tests. Maybe you are in an abusive relationship with no escape in sight or enduring a marriage gone stale. Maybe you are facing a prison term for some stupid mistake. Maybe you are just plain stuck. Maybe you are hanging on by a thread, uncertain how you're doing it, but scared out of your mind by the circumstances in which you find yourself.

This story is for you! This story is about you! Maybe you've felt that you've never needed God before. Even if you seem overwhelmed with an awful sinking feeling, face your fear and keep the faith. The only way fear can be conquered is by facing it. Avoidance brings more pain. Don't focus on the winds or the deep water. Keep your eyes fixed on Jesus and keep walking. The storms will pass. Even if you falter, God will be there to catch you!

August 11, 1996

Factions

Let there be no factions....

I Corinthians 1

——— ♥ ———

Everywhere you turn these days, people are talking about the collapse of our culture and the disintegration of commonly-held values, that glue which holds us together as churches, families, communities, and as a country. The shrill voices of fanatics at both ends of the spectrum have grabbed every microphone they can get their hands on. For fanatics, rather than seeking common ground and a respect for diversity, it's always "my way or the highway!" Community, family, church and country is possible to the degree that shared values exist. We are increasingly aware of our lack of shared values and beliefs. We find ourselves drawn more and more into the macabre national pastime of berating our various connections with each other, sliding from criticism into nit-picking into cynicism and finally into hatred.

Because negativity sells, there is a lot of plain old hysteria and paranoia folded in, but there is, nonetheless, a lot of truth in the observation that our culture may be collapsing. We really do need to wake up and take a hard look at our situation. Equally, we need to wake up and take a very hard look at the solutions being proposed by some. I am certain that not everyone agrees with me, but the idea of the recently enacted state law permitting individuals to carry concealed weapons scares the hell out of me. People will already run you down, cut you off or give you an obscene gesture in traffic if they think you are too slow, too fast or too close. What will it be like if all these stressed-out, anxious, frustrated people are carrying loaded guns under their coats? It's beginning to sound like the wild, wild West! It does look like we have taken a gigantic step backwards in our spiritual and social evolution. How did we get here? What can we do about it?

One of the biggest problems we face is our inability to reconcile and include divergent views within one frame of reference. Our country was built on the idea that people of diverse races, religions and incomes could live together by guaranteeing everyone's freedom to be different and offering everyone equal protection. This idea works when people consent to respect that basic principle. Has this become one of those shared values that is collapsing? Are we losing our ability to reconcile various views within one frame of reference? Can we have families, communities and a country without everyone having to think, act and believe alike? Is the only definition of unity we can come up with "uniformity?"

Something similar is happening within the church as well. The biggest problem facing our leadership is how to reconcile and include divergent views and still be the Catholic church. The human tendency to splinter into little cliques has always been at work against the ideal of unity. We need only read church history to know how deep this splintering has been and how often it has happened. This problem goes all the way back to the beginning. The disciples were always arguing about who was the greatest. Jesus had to break up more than one such dispute among his little band of disciples. The church in Corinth must have been a snake-pit of individualism. Corinth was a city in a high-traffic cross-roads known for its diversity of religions, cultures, philosophies and vices. The government had a hard time reconciling all this diversity, and the Christian Church there faced the same problem. Within the church, Apollos and Peter had both attracted a following. These factions each considered the other inferior. Maybe one faction was liberal and the other conservative, who knows? But they were fighting as if personal allegiance to a charismatic church leader were the "gospel." Paul reminds the believers at Corinth that their unity depended on the one essential Christ, not on clinging too tightly to non-essentials and personalities. Paul goes on to tell them that their unity is in all being Christian, not in being Paulites or Peterites or Apollonians! There was no hope of unity without a commonly-held belief in Christ. All the diversity in the church has to be subservient to this belief.

The Catholic Church, the Church whose name means to embrace and reconcile divergent non-essential views within one frame of reference, is now in crisis over how to deal with those divergent points of view. There are fanatics on the left who claim that they can no longer be part of the church unless the Pope does this or that, changes this or that, or brings things into line with their thinking. It must be done right now and let everyone who does not agree with me be cursed! There are fanatics on the right who would leave the church because the Pope is not conservative enough, having "caved in" on altar girls. One such traditionalist priest has taken a leave of absence over the altar girl issue, and will probably leave the church. Let everyone who does not agree with me be cursed! The solution? Yes, we can kill off one side or the other! Or we can focus on Christ and let go of our competition, separatism and fragments of truth. Diversity only threatens the church when our only model of unity is one of uniformity. The best Catholics are those who ignore zealots of every stripe and listen to the less shrill voices of reason and joy.

The various Christian Churches are looking for ways to be unified without strict uniformity of details. Again, any hope of reconciling and including divergent views depends on putting Christ at the center! It is Christ who makes us all Christians, whether we baptize with a cup of water or in a river-full of water! I am a Catholic by choice. I like being Catholic! I know it's not easy being Catholic today, but that's what I like about it. I am able to hold an opinion that isn't popular. I don't care if it's not stylish. I wouldn't be anything else! Nevertheless, I have a doctorate from a Presbyterian Seminary. I have worked for the United Church of Christ. I have great respect for Baptists, Quakers, Episcopalians, Pentecostals and Methodists. I started an inter-faith campus ministry program in Somerset. I helped start our own inter-faith Cathedral Heritage Foundation. That doesn't make me a weak Catholic. That doesn't mean I agree with everything believers of other traditions say or do. It does mean that I feel a unity with them that transcends any need for uniformity. I can respect and reverence these groups, can learn much from them and can preach about my choice for Roman Catholicism without putting anybody else down in the process! We certainly can be unified with our fellow Christians in other churches without agreeing on everything, or giving up our own convictions.

Our biggest problem is not that we have too many religions or opinions, but the fact that we don't live the religions we profess. As Thoreau said, "Live your beliefs and turn the world around." We must turn the world around. We must find a way to reconcile all this diversity. We must create a new idea of unity. We must find it in our country, families, churches, civic and cultural institutions. We need a definition of unity other than uniformity. We need to allow each other our convictions. We must move from a single point of view to a viewing point. From there we can keep and strengthen our own point of view with respect and reverence for other points of view!

January 21, 1996

Surviving Disappointment With Church Leaders

———— ♥ ————

Nicknames — most of us have them whether we want them or not. My family name, Knott, is an English name. It is said to be derived from the medieval English custom of calling a person with short-cropped hair a "knot" or a "knothead." Well, I've been called both. But around here let's just stick to plain old "Knott." When I was stationed in Somerset, Kentucky and was teaching sociology at the local community college, one of my students called the rectory and, in a moment of lapsed memory, asked the parish secretary, "Is, umm, is Father Bump there?" Well, I suppose "Father Knott" and "Father Bump" are pretty close together.

In today's Gospel reading, Jesus nicknames one of his disciples "Peter." (Matthew 16:13-20) Translated into English, this nickname could mean "rock" or "rocky." This disciple's real name, of course, is Simon, son of John. It was customary to give people a new name when God called them to new work, but I believe that Jesus surely had to hold back a laugh when he picked this one. It had to be tongue in cheek. Simon was anything but solid like a rock. "Sandy," as in quicksand, would be more like it. In the back of my mind I can always hear the other disciples teasing this good-hearted fisherman: "Here comes good old Rocky!"

Solid as a rock? In reality, Peter was really more a big-hearted klutz who wanted to do the right thing but usually couldn't manage to pull it off. He was forever sticking his foot in his mouth, overcompensating for the last blunder that he had made, eventually having to eat his own words. Some examples might be appropriate. One day Jesus predicted that he was going to die and that his disciples would be scattered. Well, good old Peter rushed in and bragged in front of everybody, "Listen, Lord! Even if everybody else leaves you, I will always stick with you!" A few days later it was this same Peter who said, "Jesus, who? I don't think I've ever heard of the man." (Matthew 26) It was Peter, going all out to impress Jesus with his generosity and trying to be more than twice as good as everybody else, who suggested that he would be willing to forgive another person seven times. Well, he expected Jesus to pat him on the back and say, "My, St. Peter, how wonderful you are!" Jesus says, "No, Peter, not seven times. You must forgive seventy times seven times." (Matthew 18:21-22) When Jesus is being arrested in the garden of Gethsemane, good old Peter lunged forward with his sword to save the day. He struck and, of course, he missed, cutting off a servant's ear. After the resurrection, Peter was back in his boat when he saw Jesus walking on water. Matthew's gospel says that Peter was stripped to the waist for fishing. But then the Gospel writer says Peter got so excited he put on his coat and jumped into the water. In another story, Jesus was on the shore, had prepared the fire and a grill to cook breakfast, and requested some fish. St. Peter, willing to make up for past mistakes, rushed forward and dumped one hundred fifty-three fish at the feet of Jesus. (John 21:11-13) Good old Peter! Good old Rocky!

Jesus loved Peter very much and Peter loved Jesus. Even though Peter was forever sticking his foot in his mouth and bungling everything that he touched, Peter still had a very deep faith. Stammering love is often the best love of all. One line from the Old Testament comes to mind: "People judge by externals. God sees into the heart." (1 Samuel 16:7) Or maybe the line from St. Paul: "I end up doing the things I don't want to do and find myself failing to do the things that I intend to do." (Romans 7:15)

God has always relied on thieves and idiots and prostitutes and adulterers and the handicapped to do some of the biggest and most important jobs. We might call Abraham a bigamist. Moses had a speech impediment. David was an adulterer and murderer. Jeremiah seems to whine a lot. Jonah tried to skip town. The other Simon was a middle-Eastern terrorist. Judas was a thief and a traitor. Thomas was an agnostic. James and John were politically ambitious. Mary Magdalene, we are told, was possessed by seven demons. Paul and Barnabas fought like cats and dogs on one occasion, and finally had to quit working together. But somehow God could see beyond all of their weaknesses and sins and see their goodness behind all of it. Their sheer humanity and weakness is what made them so useful to God. God has a long tradition of choosing the weak and making them strong, and of building his house with stones that other builders might reject.

What do you do when you're disappointed with the weakness of church leaders? From Archbishop Moreno to Jim Bakker, from pedophilia to embezzlement, from rumors to front page stories, it seems that every week brings yet another scandal, not only in our church but in others as well. It's not something that I enjoy talking about. I believe that it's high time that we talked about it because, no doubt, these tragedies have shaken the faith of many. I've heard people say, "Why believe anymore? They've let us down so much."

The first reason to keep believing is this: The validity of this message does not depend upon the personal goodness of the messenger. Whether it's Archbishop Moreno or Jim Bakker, they're only mediums or conduits or messengers and I hope you know that our faith is not in them. They are earthenware jars that hold a great treasure. They are not the treasure. Secondly, these people are in need of great compassion. When I go down the list of those who have fallen, one thing is obvious. They have all done good work in their lifetime. Archbishop Moreno has given many years of dedicated service to our church. He did a world of good in some very difficult situations and he rose to the top in a prejudiced church. And now he has to live with his own punishment — to live in a world that will probably remember him only for his weakest moment, not for his great moments. My heart bleeds for him. Have you ever thought of how it would feel if your deepest, darkest secrets and sins were spread on the front page of the daily newspaper next week? Worse than that, in every paper across the country? Think about it. What if **your** sins and your deep, dark secrets were put on the front page? It's scary, isn't it? And if nothing else can trigger compassion, that should. Compassion means "to suffer with," and I've often wondered when these things happen how you would react if I got into trouble. Could I depend on you for compassion? I believe that I could.

Third, the church is not the Pope, not the bishops, not your pastor or any other priest, or even Catholic lay leaders for that matter. It is a community founded by Jesus that embodies his teaching, however imperfectly. In other words, this is it! Jesus reminded us that, very often, we are like a field of weeds and wheat growing together. We're like a drag net thrown into the sea which collects all kinds of things. We are that wedding reception to which the good and the bad alike are invited. I may think that he should have known better than to pick weak human beings, but Jesus **did** know what he was doing and he did it anyway. For that reason I think that Peter the Apostle could be our hero at this time in our history. When many of Jesus' followers drifted away after the teaching on the Bread of Life, they said: "This is hard to take. Who can believe it?" I always imagine Peter standing there, confused and hurt, when Jesus finally turns to him and says, "Peter, will you go away also?" Almost pathetically, Peter responds: "I don't understand all of this, Lord. But where else can we go? You have the words of eternal life."

Fourth, we are told, and Jesus promises us, that the power of hell will not prevail against us. It's interesting that Jesus made this promise to disciples like Peter, of all people. It's obvious that Jesus prepared the church not only for the pressure that would come from the outside, but also for the pressure that would come from the inside. Maybe these built-in humility episodes that have happened recently in our church can serve to remind us all that our church leaders are not gods and to remind them that they are only earthenware jars that hold the great treasure. They are not the treasure itself. We've been through better times and, if you know your church history, you know we have certainly been through worse times. But somehow the Gospel has been handed from one generation to another, unbroken. It may be battered sometimes, but it gets through. And it will continue to get through because we are the Body of Christ, this collection of weak human beings that we call the church. Hell can't stop it, because God is with it.

143

My fellow Catholics, many of our church leaders are suffering today and because they are suffering, you are suffering. But it's hard to help others when you feel like you're bleeding to death yourself. Many priests and bishops are hurting right now. They are under great stress and when stress is combined with unbearable loneliness, it will continue to produce disastrous results. As the number of ordained clergy keeps shrinking, no doubt the pressures will rise and loneliness will increase, flushing even more stuff to the surface. I ask you to pray for us, to encourage us. We need your love and compassion.

Personally, I'm happier than I've ever been in my life. I love the excitement of a changing church. As I've said before, my goal is to stay with this and eventually to be the happiest old fart in the "Old Priests' Home." But whether I quit or whether I get thrown out or whether I get carried out in a pine box, remember one thing. The validity of the message does not depend upon the goodness of the messenger, especially this one!

August 26, 1990

On Remaining Faithful

You must remain faithful to what you have learned and believed....

2 TIMOTHY 3

———— ♥ ————

Over the years, especially in the last few years, I have received some very interesting mail. True, I've gotten a few blistering notes from some very angry people, but about ninety-nine percent of it has been extremely positive and gracious. One of the most interesting and beautiful letters was delivered week before last. It was from a woman who wanted to remain anonymous. She has been trying to find her way back to the Catholic Church after having been away for many, many years. It was more than a letter; it was a ten page long, single spaced journal. It contained some background information about her leaving, as well as a series of reflections on the homilies she has heard here over the last year. It was really a detailed account of her personal spiritual journey for the twelve months. I was amazed at the writer's dedication to her spiritual journey and flattered that she had listened so well to our preaching, taking the time to jot down her reflections. She put into words that love-hate relationship many non-practicing Catholics have with their Church. They have a "can't live with it" and "can't live without it" dilemma.

After I read this letter, it occurred to me that I have spent a lot of time and effort in the last twenty-five years helping both myself and other people remain faithful and hopeful in a less than perfect church that is, nevertheless, my true spiritual home. My correspondent's problems with the church are probably not much different from my own, except maybe in degree. I, too, struggle every day to remain faithful and hopeful.

"Remaining faithful to what we have learned and believed" is not solely a modern problem. It has always been a problem. As the Old Testament reveals, throughout their long history the people of God strayed, wandered off, got lost, fell into ruin, and had to be called back and welcomed home, over and over again. In fact, more than one prophet refers to this infidelity as "whoring around" on God. Even among the disciples of Jesus, not everybody "remained faithful to what they learned and believed." The rich young man went away sad because he could not meet the challenge. A whole slew of followers walked away from Jesus after his teaching on the Bread of Life. They just couldn't buy into it. With the exception of young John and a handful of faithful women, every one of his disciples jumped ship when Jesus was arrested.

After Jesus ascended, the young church was completely unprepared to deal with people who did not "remain faithful to what they had learned and believed." In preparation for baptism, people were rigorously trained, screened and tested for conversion of life. Baptism cleansed them of their sin and the church simply expected that these new members would never sin again, period! But when many of these believers faced being hacked or chewed to death as martyrs to the faith into which they had been baptized, some fell away, only to seek re-entry into the church at a later, safer time. The early church simply did not know how to deal with this problem. They never expected a baptized person to sin again, ever! Despite all the church's high idealism, despite all the expectations that anyone who was deeply converted in baptism had therefore forsaken all sin for the rest of their lives — still, the facts of life had set in. Baptized Christians actually committed open, public, scandalous sins. Some went back to their old pagan ways. During the persecutions some denied the faith. When some of these repented and wanted to return to the church, the church was at a loss about how to deal with them. Some argued for re-baptism, but this idea was rejected in favor of the belief that even though humans could be unfaithful to God, God could not be unfaithful to humankind. At first, the church simply excommunicated the sinners and commended them to God's mercy.

It wasn't until about 150 AD that the church offered post-baptismal forgiveness, once in a lifetime, and only after years and years of public penance. It was later, much later, that the church offered forgiveness through confession many times after baptism. Even though infidelity happened in the early church, "remaining faithful to what one had learned and believed" was a deadly serious matter.

In our second reading today, St. Paul, reading the handwriting on the wall that he is going to be beheaded soon, challenges the young Timothy "to remain faithful to what he had learned (from Paul) and believed." The Greek word there, *menein*, means to stand fast, to stay with it, to hold steady, to stick with it, to persevere. It is in this letter that Paul uses one of my favorite Greek words, *sophronismos*! Paul wishes Timothy *sophronismos*, which means "may you know what to do in the face of panic" or "May you know how to stay with it even when every bone in your body wants to run!"

I pray for *sophronismos* every day. I struggle with remaining faithful to what I have learned and believed in the church. I sometimes feel the pull to chuck it all, as so many others have done. Every time someone leaves the church, speaks disparagingly about the church or encounters something they don't like in the church and tells me about it, my foundations are shaken. I am forced to ask myself what I believe, why I am still here and what do I have faith in, anyway? I have always had a soft spot in my heart for people who have drifted away because I have sometimes been sorely tempted myself.

What I tell them is what I tell myself. (1) Remember, your faith is not in the institution. Your faith is in the Holy Spirit living in the church who will be with it until the end of time. (2) As pitiful as the institution is on some days and as much as we would like to experience only the parts we like best, like kids eating the filling out of the Oreo and throwing away the rest, we can't. The church **is** the Body of Christ in the world and we can't have Christ without dealing with his church, all his messy people! We can't be like the Peanuts comic strip character Lucy who once announced: "I love humanity — it's people I can't stand!" We can't say we love Christ and at the same time hate his body, the church. I'm sorry, but it can't be just "me and Jesus," no matter how badly we may want it!

(3) You don't have to like everything going on in the church to "remain faithful" to it! There is no perfect church. There never has been! Grow up and get over it! If the church were perfect, it would probably run us off, anyway! Thank God the church isn't perfect, I'd hate to stand out like a sore thumb!

To all who have left the church for a while and have returned, or seek to return, I say welcome! Sometimes we have to leave something before we can examine it again with new eyes and a new heart. Leaving can actually be a blessing in disguise. It can actually make us stronger in the faith. Many of the great saints wandered away and found their way back: Peter, Thomas, Augustine, Francis of Assisi. The tragedy of Judas was not that he denied Christ, not that he left the company of disciples, but that he could neither forgive himself nor accept forgiveness. He gave up.

This parish is full of people who came back to the church, came back and rediscovered a stronger faith and practice than they ever had before they left. They are lectors, eucharistic ministers, teachers, social service volunteers, musicians and committee chairs. They are old and young, married and single, rich and poor. Sometimes leaving is about sorting things out. Sometimes leaving enables us to shed a simplistic childhood faith to make room for a more conscious, adult faith. An adult faith is not something that happens **to** us. It is something to which we must be open — something we must really want. Adult faith is about taking responsibility for one's own spiritual growth, rather than excusing oneself from that work by blaming crude and crusty clerics, obnoxious nuns or defective parents of one's childhood. An adult faith can handle the fact that the church has a sinful side. An adult faith remains faithful to what was learned and believed, in spite of the messiness of trying to live out that faith among flawed people. An adult faith does not blame; it accepts responsibility. An adult faith transcends the pettiness of human weaknesses, even in the church.

October 22, 1995

149

An Apostolic Church: Built On A Rock

. . . on this rock I will build my church and the gates of hell will not prevail against it.

MATTHEW 16

———— ♥ ————

I have lived under five Popes! Several years back, I had a chance to travel to Rome and visit the tombs of four of those five Popes in the undercroft of St. Peter's Basilica. I was so moved by the experience that I went back again the next day. Back in the corner was Pope Pius XII. He was Pope when I was baptized, learned my prayers, made my first communion and was confirmed. He was stoic, stern and serious. Over on a side wall was Pope John XXIII. I was thirteen years old and in my first year of high school seminary when he was elected. He was a charmer. Everybody felt that they knew him personally. He is the Pope I would most like to have met. He made me believe in the Holy Spirit.

Over to one side of him was Pope Paul VI, the only one buried below ground. He was Pope when I studied theology, prepared for priesthood and was ordained. He accomplished a lot and suffered much. He seemed to agonize over everything. I have come to respect and admire him more and more as the years go by. When I left his tomb, I whispered, "Thanks!"

Out in the middle of the floor, almost in the way, was Pope John Paul I in a huge box of shiny new marble slabs, trimmed with ornate old marble artifacts. I was pastor of my first parish when he was elected. He only lasted a few weeks, but during that brief time he earned the nickname the "Smiling Pope." I will always wonder what the church might be like today if he had lived. I was in a room full of Protestant ministers in Cincinnati when the election of Pope John Paul II was announced. I have served most of the years of my priesthood under this Pope. He is a man of iron principle in a world of compromise. He has presided over the most divided church in recent history. I feel sorry for him. It seems the harder he tries, the more divided we get! He looks tired, worried and worn. He is aging, moving toward the end of his pontificate. Within a few years, the 265th successor of St. Peter will be elected to take John Paul II's place and the church will continue.

This is a critical time in the Church. Divisions are so sharp that if you dare read the liberal newspaper *National Catholic Reporter (NCR)* and watch the conservative television program "Mother Angelica Live," you risk inducing a serious episode of religious schizophrenia. The papacy of Pope John Paul II inspires pride, hope and trust for some; bitter disappointment, even anger, in others. People are already saying that what we need from the next Pope will be the ability to reconcile various parts of the church, dizzy from change and bruised from infighting.

But when has it been otherwise in the history of the church? It was like this even during St. Peter's tenure. No sooner had Peter made his profession of faith and Jesus declared him the "rock" on which he will build his church, we find Jesus saying to him, "Get out of my sight, you have the thoughts of a Satan,"

152

Peter's leadership was sprinkled with bragging, denials, betrayals, reconciliations, victories, arguments with Paul and disappointment with his own people. Following Peter's tenure, his office has often neared disaster. The papacy has survived the meddling of imperial armies, the dark ages, the infidelities of monks, the scandals of Popes, the wounds of schism, religious wars, the sale of bishoprics, to name only a few of the challenges. Yet doom is not our destiny. We continue, in spite of infidelities, diminishment and failure. We have the promise of Christ that we will survive and that even the gates of hell shall not prevail against us.

In our Creed, that sacred summary of our faith we recite each Sunday, we Catholics say that we "believe in one, holy, catholic and apostolic church." In other words, we believe that we have an inherited faith, a faith connected across the centuries by the visible sign of the successor of Peter, the Pope, and the successors of the apostles, our bishops. Today, I want to talk to you about the papal office and its role in our church, as well as about the present occupant for whom the priest prays at each and every Mass; the one he says we are "in union with;" prayers to which we all assent by saying: "Amen!"

The sharp divisions in the church are scandalous. We are beginning to treat the Pope like some kind of American political candidate. People of divergent perspectives talk about each other as if they were enemies. We can each have our favorite Pope, but we must not destroy the office of the successor of St. Peter just because we may not personally agree with the policies of the one who currently holds that office. The office is our connection to the past. It's what makes us an apostolic church. Let's not throw the baby out with the bath water. Let's not cut off our noses to spite our faces. Those who disagree must always be, at the very least,

153

a loyal opposition. Let us view the Pope with eyes of compassion. It is his awesome task to govern the universal church, not like a popularity contest, but in fidelity to the truth as he sees it. When all is said and done, I would rather trust him to guide the church than any of the columnists in the *NCR* or any of the guests on all the talk shows on television. If we destroy this essential symbol of unity and orthodoxy, we run the risk of disintegrating into a host of special interest cults. We will lose our catholicity and our universality. Some, in a blind rage, confuse a need for Vatican reform with the destruction of our sacred religious heritage. With patience, faith, prayer and perseverance, the church can work through its problems and make wise changes as it sifts the grain from the chaff.

I realize this is hard to accept for people who are used to instant gratification. American Catholics, in particular, tend to forget that our agenda and timetable are not necessarily the agenda and timetable of the whole church.

There are many changes I would like to see in our church and I realize that I may not get my way on many issues, but I don't need to take my toys and go home. I am very proud to be a part of an apostolic church, proud to be part of something bigger than me and my opinions, proud to be part of something that will be around longer than I am. The church, in the final analysis, will get better by the personal conversion of life of individual members, not by destroying our sacred traditions. There is enough within ourselves that needs to be fixed to keep us all busy for years to come. Pray for the church. Pray for our leaders. Keep the faith!

August 21, 1996

Mud And Stars

...the chief priests and elders came to Jesus as he was teaching and challenged his authority.

MATTHEW 21

——— ♥ ———

With all the news coverage, you surely know by now that several priests in the archdiocese, including myself, received a sad little book in the mail last week from an anonymous group of archconservative Catholics. It arrived in a plain brown wrapper, unsigned, with no return address. The authors call it a "white paper." It is, for the most part, a hate-filled collection of personal attacks, half-truths, exaggerations, embellishments, distortions and even a few lies. The material was gathered by a small army of clandestine reporters, sent out secretly to visit various parishes around the archdiocese, for the explicit purpose of documenting so-called abuses and deviations by priests and parishes they don't like, understand, or with whom they do not agree. Several pages are directed at me personally, my book of homilies, the Cathedral Parish, the Cathedral renovation and the Cathedral Heritage Foundation.

In short, they hate about everything we have done here in the last thirteen years. It is obvious that the authors are completely overwhelmed with fear and believe that a return to some kind of idealized pre-Vatican II church, when everything was wonderful, is the only solution. The white paper reeks of that same old "them and us," "we're right and you're wrong" thinking that has infected politics and churches, synagogues and mosques all around the world. This kind of thinking leads to seeing enemies, real or imagined. It is a strain of intolerant religious thinking that, left unchecked, has led to many of the violent religious bloodbaths we hear about on the news every night these days.

All this gave me a little more insight into what Jesus was up against in today's gospel story from St. Matthew. We see this kind of thinking played out in the ministry of Jesus almost 2,000 years ago. Jesus had been doing great things among the prostitutes, sinners and marginal people of his time. He had Gentile friends. He had befriended them, taught them and even defended them against the vicious attacks and sanctimonious piety of certain members of his religious community. The chief priests and the elders didn't like what he was doing. They didn't like it one bit! The more successful Jesus was among these people, the more determined the authorities were to stop him. The chief elders and priests believed that the so-called "sinners" and Gentiles to whom Jesus reached out needed to be condemned and shunned, not embraced and befriended. They believed that Jesus was teaching a notion of God's love which was too lenient. For the good of religion, Jesus needed to be stopped.

In response to the criticism of the religious leadership, Jesus tells them a little story. The point of his little parable about two sons is that both the so-called "sinners" and those who judge them have a long way to go. The Jewish religious authorities are the son who brags about obeying God and really didn't. The tax collectors and prostitutes are the son who said he would go his own way and then took God's way. The key to correct understanding of this parable is that it is not really praising either son: both were unsatisfactory. Neither son, in the parable, was the kind of son to bring full joy to his father, even though the one who in the end responded to Jesus was the better of the two bad sons. The ideal son would be the son who accepted his father's orders with obedience and respect and who unquestioningly and fully carried them out.

The parable reminds us that there are those in the church whose profession is much better than their practice. They make great claims to piety and fidelity, but are often filled with anger, hate, fear and judgment. This parable also reminds us that there are those who know their sins and feel the condemning sting of the self-righteous, but who sometimes live more authentically Christian lives than those doing the condemning. The parable ends with Jesus looking the condemners right in the eye and delivering this devastating indictment. "Truly, I tell you" is a way of saying "Listen up!" "Listen up, you! Tax collectors and prostitutes are going into the kingdom of God ahead of you." No wonder they wanted to attack him. No wonder the authorities wanted to kill him. No wonder they did! The message here is simple. We both have a long way to go — those who are condemned and those who do the condemning.

Regardless of the recent attacks, I know who I am and I know who you are. I know that I am consciously Christian, deliberately Roman Catholic and unapologetically ecumenical. I know that I am unequivocally committed to the Roman Catholic Church. I know that my faith in Jesus Christ is solid. I know that my Catholic faith has been strengthened, not weakened, by trying to understand the faith of others. I know that I have given my very best to the church

157

as a priest for twenty-six years now and that I plan to continue to give it my best until God calls me home. I also know that you are very good and holy people. I know that you are not looking for some easy religion. I know that you want to be challenged. I know that you are proud of what we have been able to do to bring this place back to life. I know that we have been able to welcome back hundreds of so-called "fallen away" Catholics who otherwise would have been lost to the Catholic Church.

I know that the Cathedral Heritage Foundation is working creatively and courageously to promote understanding and respect among the religions of our community, in a world where religious fanatics are killing each other because they cannot tolerate any point of view other than their own. I know that the Cathedral Heritage Foundation is not asking any religion to compromise its theology, especially Roman Catholics. I know the very opposite to be true. I know that the Cathedral Heritage Foundation is interested in the spiritual growth of Catholics as well as the spiritual growth of all people of good will. I know that the Cathedral Heritage Foundation is actually doing more than most Catholic organizations, for that matter, to preserve and celebrate the Catholic heritage of this very place. I also know that many of you who are living with circumstances that you didn't choose, be it a divorce or a sexual orientation, and that you are doing the very best you know how to respond to God. I know that you do not want the church to lower its high standards, but simply to offer a safe place, without abuse and harsh condemnation, where you can grow spiritually regardless of your circumstances.

I know for a fact that God is alive around here, that God is alive and active in your lives and mine, that God is not just a word in some rule book. I know you to be faith-filled and generous people who are proud to be Catholic, whether you are the kids who sing in our choir, the families who feed the poor, the hundreds who serve so faithfully in liturgical ministries, the office workers who pray here everyday or the elderly who encourage and support us priests through thick and thin.

Our critics remind me of an old poem that goes something like this:

> Two men looked out from prison bars.
> One saw mud, the other saw stars.

No, we are not perfect, but we have enough of which to be proud to fill a book a hundred times bigger than their mean little publication. The white paper could have mentioned the fact that we have grown from almost being closed down to becoming one of the largest parishes in the archdiocese in thirteen short years. It could have mentioned that we have choirs that can sing the best versions of *Panis Angelicus* and *Ave Maria* that has been heard in this city for a long time. It could have mentioned the hundreds of volunteers who feed thousands of street people from our doors, in all kinds of weather, every day of the year. It could have mentioned my homily on respecting the teaching authority of the Pope last month or our parish Lenten retreat, "Consciously Christian, Deliberately Catholic." It could have mentioned the more two hundred adults who have enrolled in our new School of Catholic Spiritual Growth and Education. These parishioners will be dragging themselves downtown at night and on Saturdays, to study the ancient spiritual disciplines of fasting, prayer, personal reflection, almsgiving, and spiritual reading for sixteen hours over eight weeks. The white paper could have mentioned our fast-growing youth group, young adult group, seniors group and singles group. It could have mentioned the hundreds of "fallen away" Catholics who have returned to the Sacraments. It could have celebrated, rather than attacked, the patient and generous contributions of hundreds of wonderful women around here. It could have mentioned the national and regional architectural and preservation awards our renovation has won. The white paper could have mentioned thousands of good things, both here and in the parishes it condemns, but sadly, all they see is mud!

This little book may aggravate, but it will not dissuade. In fact, every time we are attacked we go through another growth spurt. I thank all of you who are making all these good things happen. I thank all of you for the personal support you have given and continue to give both me and Father Marty. Let's put this attack in perspective. Let's take it for what it is: the hatching of a small number of fear-filled minds. Let's not make them our enemies in return. Let's wish them well. Let's honor the work of places like St. Louis Bertrand as well as Epiphany, St. Martin as well as St. Pius. And let's get back to the great work of building a spiritual center in downtown Louisville.

My fellow Catholics, there is a lot of "mud" in the world today, but I challenge you to look up and see the stars!

September 29, 1996

"Forgive Us As We Forgive Others" — Be Careful What You Ask For

Wrath and anger are hateful things, yet the sinner hugs them tight. Should a person nourish anger against his fellows and expect healing from the Lord?

SIRACH 27:30

———— ♥ ————

About four years ago, a friend of mine tried to talk me into adopting a dog. Even though I resisted for a long time, my friend finally wore me down and, in a moment of weakness, I said I would try it. Big mistake. It lasted six days. I couldn't take it.

He was as big as a horse, an English sheep dog! His name was Bear. He was the most affectionate dog I have ever been around in my life. He craved affection. He was a bona fide affection addict. Every time I came home, I had to fight my way through the door with one huge paw on each shoulder. Bear loved to sit in the middle of the floor and stare at me. As I moved from room to room, he followed, sat down, panted and stared. Do you realize how wearisome it is to be licked on and stared at from daylight to dark, especially for a person who is used to living alone? I couldn't take it!

One of the funniest things Bear did was to come to my bedroom every morning and lay down beside the bed about five minutes before the alarm went off. He would place his nose about four inches from my ear and sniff until I woke up. The last straw was that Bear got so lonely while I was gone for twelve hours he started chewing up the furniture. For my sanity and his, I had to let him go!

St. Peter was a lot like my dog, Bear. Poor thing! He craved approval and affection from Jesus and, like a little puppy, was always trying to come up with some new way to get it. The harder he tried, the more Peter fell on his face. He was always missing the mark. He had a serious case of "foot in mouth." He was a big klutz with a big heart! We see him in action again in today's gospel. Peter had just heard Jesus give a sermon on what to do when someone sins against you. Peter saw an opportunity for a pat of approval. His little mind was really working overtime here. He so desperately wanted to impress Jesus. The gospel says that Peter "came to Jesus." Peter had obviously been rehearsing a little scenario. He asked Jesus a question and then turned around and answered his own question. "How many times must I forgive? Seven?" Peter knew very well what the rabbis taught, that a person needed to forgive only three times. Peter doubled that and added one. Seven! He obviously expected Jesus to say: "Wow, Peter! How generous you are!" What Jesus said instead was: "Peter, don't even keep count! Seventy times seven does not mean four hundred ninety times. It means that one must forgive every time, no matter how many times it takes! That's how God does it! Be like God when it comes to forgiveness! Fump! Peter — you missed again!"

162

Jesus used this opportunity to teach Peter about forgiveness by telling him a little story about a man who was forgiven a $25,000,000 debt, then turned around and refused to forgive a $100 debt that was owed to him. The point is this: We are hopelessly in debt to God. God simply absolves the whole debt — wipes the slate clean. God only asks that we do the same for each other! If we don't, it's our loss. We cannot appreciate and experience God's forgiveness unless we open the channel clogged by our lack of forgiveness of others.

One of the most dangerous prayers we utter is the Lord's Prayer. We actually ask God to "forgive us as we forgive others." It is backed up by another quote from Jesus: "The measure you use to measure others will be used to measure you!"

Who are the people in your life whom you have not forgiven? An ex-spouse? One of your kids? One of your parents? A sister or brother? An old boss? A former roommate? An old teacher, a priest, religious sister or brother? A neighbor? Who are the people in your life whom you have not forgiven? Forgiveness is not optional in the Christian life. It is what being a Christian is all about. We do not have a choice. We can hold our hurts and nurture them, hug our resentments, project our frustrations outward, carry a stinking bag of excuses for not being happy. For me it was my father. Until I was in my mid-thirties I carried around a ugly bundle of resentment and blame toward him, even while I preached well-received sermons on God's unconditional forgiveness. I was talking to others about forgiveness. Sometimes the words of the Lord's Prayer would stick in my throat, because there I was — a priest who could not forgive his own father!

Meditation, prayer and study are necessary parts of the process. When I finally wanted to forgive, I still couldn't. I began to pray for help. I asked God to change my heart. I listened to tapes and read books and articles on forgiveness, compassion and reconciliation.

If you continue to pray, meditate and study, you can be sure an opportunity will appear. A road will open up and you will be invited to walk it. About six months after making the decision to forgive my father, I finally made my move. Something, indeed, had shifted in my heart.

I believe you need some kind of external, symbolic expression. I decided that I needed to tell my father face-to-face just how angry I had been at him, but that this time I needed to do it without all the venom and anger. I set up a dinner. At the end of the dinner, I told him how angry I had felt toward him for years, but also told him that I wanted to get beyond it. I really meant it. I forgave him in my heart and I asked for my father's forgiveness for years of cold-shouldered punishment I had meted out to him. I had never felt that good in my whole life.

Who in your life have you yet to forgive? Are you sick of being mad — sick of rehearsing the same old refrain of "he said - she said?" I would be thrilled if I could persuade even one or two of you to look into the benefits of unilateral and unconditional forgiveness. Imagine how much lighter you could feel if you could let go of that stinking, heavy bag of garbage called "unforgiveness." Believe me, carrying it around isn't worth it! God wants you to forgive, not for his benefit, but for yours! He wants you to be free of it. God invites you to let go of your grip on the person you wanted another to be, and to accept others simply as they are. Forgive them, no matter how many hurts you carry. It's hard to do, but it's worth it and you can do it with God's help. It takes a lot of energy to keep an enemy. Use that energy to get on with your life. With a heart cleared of all that garbage, you can celebrate the unconditional love and forgiveness that God has for you!

September 15, 1996

The Good News
(And The Bad News)
About Being "Blessed" By God

Blessed are you among women and blessed is the fruit of your womb. Blessed is she who trusted that the Lord's words to her would be fulfilled.

LUKE 1

———— ♥ ————

Back when I was a young parish priest, while I was associate pastor at St. Mildred Parish in Somerset, I designed several large banners for the church. The people seemed to appreciate most of them, but one of them raised more than one old lady's eyebrows. It pictured a very pregnant Mary, sitting in a rocking chair deep in meditation, her arms folded carefully over her swollen abdomen. I was trying to capture the words of the gospel in the Annunciation story: "Mary was deeply troubled by the angel's words and wondered what his greeting meant." I tried to imagine Mary sitting around her house trying to figure out what all this meant and where her life would lead. After all, she was an unwed mother in the eyes of the Jewish law! Well, the banner was a little blasphemous in the eyes of some of the very pious. But I stood my ground and it went up every year while I was there. They finally got used to it and many came to love it.

In the first chapter of Luke, Mary is called "blessed" no fewer than three times, once by the angel Gabriel and twice by her cousin Elizabeth. "Blessedness" is not all peaches and cream, not by a long shot. Mary was granted the blessedness of being the mother of the Son of God. Her heart was filled with both joy and sorrow because of this blessedness. This blessedness was also to be a sword to pierce her heart. It meant that someday she would see her son hanging on a cross, spit at, and despised by the crowds.

To be chosen and blessed by God has its ups and downs. It means great joy and it means great sorrow. Ask anyone who has ever had such a vocation! Ask Peter, Paul, John the Baptist, any of the martyrs, Theresa, Augustine, Joseph, Abraham and Sarah, Jeremiah, Jonah or Isaiah. Ask any of the millions of parents, priests and sisters — anyone who has been called by God for some special task. The raw truth is that God does not choose a person for ease and comfort, but to use that person for his special designs and purposes. To be called by God is a scary adventure. With the privilege goes awesome responsibility. Nowhere can we better see the paradox of blessedness than in the life of Mary. She had the joy of being the mother of the Son of God, but she also had to face the ridicule of her neighbors, the possibility of being abandoned by Joseph, the disappearance of Jesus for three days when he was a boy, the possibility that he had lost his mind when he was a young rabbi and, finally, his cruel and tortured death when he was a young man.

Mary was "blessed" alright. But the gospels honor her not so much for her unique and privileged position as "mother" as for her total trust in God, no matter what! "I am the servant of the Lord. Let it be done to me as you say." As

168

the privileged mother, we can admire her. As one who totally trusts God, in good times and bad, we can emulate her!

Like Mary's "blessedness," this holiday season is a confusing mixture of joy and sadness. I have heard story after story of happy engagements, heroic generosity, new babies, families being reunited, reconciliations among old enemies, beautiful celebrations and jobs found. But I have also heard a lot of sad stories about unemployment, terrible sicknesses, old people in nursing homes who cannot die, broken marriages, family fights and auto accidents. In fact, being "blessed" by God means, for me, absorbing these stories. One minute I will get a letter from a parishioner who tells me how much closer he or she has drawn to God by being part of the Cathedral; the next minute the phone rings telling me about a newly discovered cancer or upcoming surgery. One minute I am going to a Christmas party; the next minute I am on my way to my uncle's funeral in Brandenburg. One morning I am stopped by somebody on the street who gushes with compliments about the new Cathedral; at mid-afternoon I get a call from a neighboring pastor whose parishioner who wants to circulate a petition condemning me for "letting all those heretical religions use the Cathedral." One hour I get a call telling me that I am to receive an award for community building; the next hour I am viciously castigated by a fundamentalist for putting those "secular statues" out in front of the church. Most evenings, when it all quiets down and I am alone with my thoughts, I just sit in a big chair and wonder what it all means. Some evenings, I don't know whether to laugh or cry. Like Mary in her rocking chair in that banner I designed years ago, I just sit and wonder what it all means and where it will all lead. Like Mary kneeling before the angel Gabriel, I also hear the words "do not fear," "God is at work here," "trust God, believe in yourself and dare to dream."

My friends, on this fourth Sunday of Advent, the church holds Mary up as a model of complete trust in God, in good times and in bad, through thick and thin. Many of us have gotten the impression that problems, pain and disappointment are signs of God's absence. Mary teaches us today that all the confusion of joy and sorrow is actually a sign of "blessedness," a sign that God is indeed active and even the terrible things can be turned to good.

My friends, don't let Advent go by this year without a few minutes in a rocking chair with Mary, praying over what it all means. Advent is a time to renew our commitment to trust God no matter what, and patiently wait for insight into what it all means! Those who are suffering this holiday season, do not lose heart! The Lord is with you!

December 18, 1994

Christians

. . . it was in Antioch that the disciples were first called Christians.

ACTS 11

——— ♥ ———

hristian! St. Luke tells us that the followers of Jesus were called "Christians" for the first time at Antioch. It was a nickname, a nickname spoken in voices that dripped with contempt. "Those Christians!" In the centuries since then, millions of heroic men and women have given life and limb for that name. But millions of others have used that name to perpetuate some of the world's worst atrocities.

Christian! Under that name men and women of faith have built grand cathedrals, founded great universities, written magnificent music, produced great paintings and sculptures, written timeless literature. Under that name men and women of faith have started great religious orders to serve the world's poor through their hospitals, schools and orphanages, celebrated faith-filled liturgies and watered the church with their martyrs' blood and tears of compassion.

Christian! In the thirteenth century, church leaders were so concerned about the purity of the Christian faith that they instituted a process (called the Inquisition) to deal harshly with unwanted expressions and activities in the church. The Inquisition continued over several centuries. Inquisitors hunted people down, subjecting them to interrogation and even torture. Suspects could be imprisoned for years. Those convicted of heresy could be burned, hanged, drowned or cut into quarters. Whole towns could be punished. Between five million and fifteen million people lost their lives at the hands of these "Christian" fanatics. These "Christians" believed they were protecting Christianity by ridding the church of its impurities.

Certain "Christians" in every age have rationalized torture and death as necessary for the preservation of "truth." The long and bloody Crusades against Moslems and Jews were always carried out under the highest spiritual motives. Their motto was: "God wills it!" We still pay for some of their atrocities. During Reformation times, Luther condoned killing peasants who revolted. Calvin had Servetus burned at the stake. Cromwell killed in the name of the Lord. New England Puritans sought out and burned "witches." Queen Mary killed Protestants. Queen Elizabeth killed Catholics. They claimed they did it to "protect" the Christian faith!

What is the lesson here? Just because something springs from a group calling itself "Christian" does not make it Christian! This has been true in the past. It is true today! There are "Christians" today who can justify almost any horrible means as necessary for the preservation of their "truth." Look at all the religious wars going on around the world at this very minute. In our own country, fanatics don't necessarily leave visible marks on their victims. They simply ruin them through innuendo, anonymous letters, slander and gross exaggeration. The so-called "Christian Right" worries me terribly in this regard. One recent political victor in Texas, who won with the help of the Christian Coalition, favors executing homosexuals. At another Christian

172

political conference last year, two thousand people stood with a former Vice President and recited "I pledge allegiance to the Christian flag..." Some can even justify in their own minds shooting doctors who perform abortions as a way to protest against abortion. Read your church history and keep your eye on these people! Just because it springs from a group calling itself "Christian" does not make it Christian! "By their fruits you shall know them!"

What does it mean to be "Christian" in its purest sense? Look not to fanatics, crusaders and inquisitionists! Look to today's gospel for that answer. What we have here is an outline of basic and fundamental Christianity.

To be "Christian" is to be Christ-like. To be Christ-like is to be radically generous, radically loving, radically forgiving and radically compassionate. "Love your enemies. Do good to those who hate you. Bless those who curse you and pray for those who mistreat you. Be compassionate. Do not judge. Do not condemn. Pardon. Give. The measure you measure with will be measured back to you." This is what it means to be a Christian! If God can be good to the ungrateful and the wicked, as Jesus says in today's gospel, then "Christians" can never quit doing the same! Those who live this way "will rightly be called sons and daughters of the Most High." Christian is as Christian does! It is not those who say "Lord, Lord," but those who do the will of God!

Christianity has always had its merchants of hate, those people who claim the name, but don't really believe today's gospel. Loving enemies? Turning the other cheek? Being compassionate? Not judging and condemning? Pardoning and forgiving? They don't really believe it works! They really believe all that stuff is naive and totally impractical. In essence, they don't really believe in the basic Christian mes-

173

sage. But in the end, this "good news" will always be more powerful than their bad news!

Want to be a real Christian? Put **this** into everyday practice! "Be compassionate, as your Father is compassionate. Do not judge, and you will not be judged. Do not condemn, and you will not be condemned. Pardon, and you will be pardoned. Give, and it will be given to you. Good measure pressed down, shaken together, running over, shall they pour into the fold of your garment. For the measure you measure with will be measured back to you." (Luke 6:36-38)

February 19, 1995

Prophets: People Who Rub Our Noses in the Truth

———— ♥ ————

I can hear my mother now. "If it were a snake, it would have bitten you!" That was her way of saying, "It's right there in front of you, right under your nose!" Throughout my childhood she used to send me to find something in the kitchen drawers, like the beaters for the hand mixer. I'd rummage and rummage until she would walk over, huffing in exasperation, and pick them out of the drawer where the beaters rested in plain sight, right in front of me! I can hear her now, saying as she shook her head: "Ronnie, if it were a snake it would have bitten you!"

There are some of us who have no eyesight because of some accident or eye disease. There are others of us who have perfect eyesight, but absolutely no insight. We can look right at things and see nothing! There are still others of us who have perfect eyesight, but choose not to see.

Ophthalmologists and schools for the blind can help people who have no eyesight. Teachers can help people who just don't "get it." But only prophets can help people who don't want to see! Contrary to what most people think, prophets are not people who predict what will be going on in the future nearly as much as they are people who can see clearly what in going on in the present. Prophets are not so much people of foresight as they are people of insight. They are people who rub our noses in the truth of present situations, whether we want to see or not!

Prophets rock the boat. They stir up the dust. They make trouble. They disturb sleeping dogs. They make us look at the truth "right under our noses." They will let neither individuals nor groups doze off! Because prophets tend to force us to look at truths we would rather not see, most prophets end up getting killed. Prophets are killed not because they have lied about something, but because they have told the truth to somebody who did not want to hear it!

John the Baptist was such a man. He had insight and he told the truth. First of all, John pointed out the presence of God in the person of Jesus in the midst of the people! All the crowd saw when they looked at Jesus was a young Jewish man from Nazareth! John saw God's Son. That's what prophets do; they point out the presence of God to us when they recognize it. John, second of all, confronted Herod bluntly with his own wrong doing. John got up in Herod's face and told him, "Herod, the way you are living is wrong. You're living with your brother's wife!" That's what prophets do; they rub our noses in the truth. John the Baptist was not beheaded because he lied, but because he told the truth to a man who didn't want to hear spoken aloud what his conscience had already told him.

Because the truth sometimes hurts and we try to avoid the pain, God has provided two correctives. God created inside truth-tellers called "consciences" and outside truth-tellers called "prophets." Conscience is that inner voice, that built-in truth-teller that accuses us when we lie either to ourselves or others. The ancient prophet, Isaiah, described it in these words centuries ago: "While from behind, a voice shall sound in your ears: 'This is the way; walk in it,' when you would turn to the right or to the left." (Isaiah 30:21 NAB) Conscience reminds us of the truth even when we go against it, try to deaden it or flat out refuse to listen to it. Conscience exposes lies, especially those we tell ourselves. Conscience can be ignored, dulled and blinded over time by a habitual disregard for truth and goodness, just so we can do what we want, when we want to do it. Not only can conscience be deadened slowly over time, it can, like a truth-telling prophet, be killed completely. Some Catholics not only want to do wrong, they even insist that the church re-write the rules so they can feel good about doing wrong. This is not just happening among adults. Therapists and social service professionals have now identified a frightening new epidemic among children. As a result of a sickening pattern of child abuse and child neglect, we have produced a generation of children of whom a staggering percentage are inwardly isolated and emotionally unapproachable. They have been called "children without consciences." Of course, this is not a majority of children, but these "children without consciences" may now make up as much as fifteen percent of the population.

Because we have this human ability to lie to ourselves and to fall for the lies of others, even to the point of numbing our consciences, God has also sent truth-telling prophets to serve as our outside consciences. Prophets are people who hold us to our principles. Prophets are sent to expose lies; those lies we tell ourselves, and those lies we conspire with others to tell. Because we want to do what we want to do, we beat, silence, jail, excommunicate, shun, exile and even murder the voices of those who dare challenge us. We murder the messenger because we don't like the message.

177

My friends, people who tell us what we want to hear, making us feel good for a while, are a dime a dozen, but they are not necessarily our friends. People who tell us what is hard to hear, making us feel bad for a while, are as scarce as hen's teeth, but they are not necessarily our enemies. Sometimes those who love us most are those who challenge our bad behaviors. Sometimes those who love us least ignore or even encourage us in our bad behaviors.

Lying to ourselves and lying to each other are big problems in our world today and the effect of all this dishonesty is catching up with us, in spades! If you don't believe me, just watch the constant stream of lying, unprincipled and pathetic people who are paraded out everyday on almost every TV talk show! The world desperately needs people who listen to their consciences. The world desperately needs people who pay heed to their prophets.

"The truth will make you free," Jesus says. He might have said, "The truth will make you free, but first it will aggravate the hell out of you." Yes, the truth hurts. That's why we try so hard to get around it. We may choose blindness, ignorance and comfort over truth, but truth is extremely powerful. Truth will triumph in the end. In the meantime, for our own good, our consciences will continue to speak up with what we need to hear in the quiet moments of our lives. For our own good, prophets will be sent by God to aggravate us, to challenge us and to remind us of the truth, even when we are lying through our teeth either to ourselves or to the people around us!

December 14, 1997
preached at Saint Theresa and Saint Mary Magdalen de Pazzi Churches in Meade County, Kentucky

Choosing Wisely

Wisdom is radiant and unfading and she is easily discerned by those who love her and is found by those who seek her. She goes about seeking those worthy of her and she graciously appears to them in their paths and meets them in every thought.

WISDOM 6

— ♥ —

Do you want what's behind door number one, door number two or door number three? Do you want to keep the new kitchen appliances that you have already won or do you want to trade them for what's behind the curtain on stage? Many of you remember the long-running TV show, "Let's Make A Deal." Contestants in ridiculous costumes were offered choices between a bird in the hand or two in the bush, between what was certain and what was possible. Sometimes people would trade something like a plastic comb for a choice of three doors. Sometimes they would end up with a Hawaiian vacation and sometimes with a booby prize. Sometimes they were confronted with a second choice. They were asked whether they wanted to trade their Hawaiian vacation for what's behind a curtain. They might then win a new car or lose their vacation and end up with a jackass. The program was popular, I believe, because it was symbolic of the human predicament. We are faced with a world of choices and sometimes our choices produce great blessings and sometimes they lead to disaster. Sometimes we are better off because of our choices and sometimes we have to live in a hell of regret, knowing that we brought ruin on ourselves because of our bad choices.

Making good choices requires not merely knowledge, but wisdom. We live in a world of unprecedented knowledge on one hand and an unprecedented lack of wisdom on the other. We have a whole lot of smart people doing a whole lot of dumb things. We know a lot of facts and we have a lot of information at our disposal. At the same time, we are knee-deep in the fallout from people's bad choices.

Freedom to choose from a smorgasbord of choices does not guarantee that we choose wisely. God says in the Book of Deuteronomy, "Today I set before you life and death, a blessing and a curse. Choose life!" Why, then, do we so often choose death and the curse? The first thing we were taught in theology was that there is a world of difference between knowledge and wisdom. That's why people with advanced degrees in theology don't always make the best preachers, why people with doctorates in music don't always make the best music ministers, why the best seminarians don't always make the best priests. That's why a nation of well-educated people like ours can be so full of pain and confusion. Wisdom is knowledge integrated with experience. Wisdom is knowledge tested in reality. That's why wisdom usually comes with age and experience, if it comes at all.

Even though our first reading was written over two thousand years ago, it is remarkably fresh and useful today because the times in which we live are, in many ways, similar to the times in which its author lived. It was written in Egypt by an unknown writer who lived in the last half of the first century before Christ. Whoever he was, he was a learned,

Greek speaking Jew, probably a teacher, who was familiar with Greek philosophy, rhetoric and culture. The Book of Wisdom is one of those books in our Bible which is not included in Protestant Bibles. The Book of Wisdom is one man's summary of years of devoted study. It is the wisdom gleaned from all the Sacred Literature of the Jews and applied to his situation, giving hope and consolation to his contemporaries. He wrote to strengthen the faith of his fellow Jews living in Alexandria, Egypt. They lived amidst pagans. They lived at a time of scientific conquests that were opening up to the people the beauty and mystery of the world around them. They lived in a society that had a variety of religions and philosophical systems offering salvation and answers to the meaning of life. His society was individualistic, skeptical and dissatisfied with traditional ideas. It was a time of crisis for the faith, which some Jews had abandoned and replaced with pagan religions and secular philosophies. It was to people living in this situation that the author addressed himself, having searched the Scriptures for solutions. The Book of Wisdom is addressed to students and intellectuals and reminded them that they did not need to envy the wisdom of the pagans around them because they possessed true wisdom, the wisdom of God. But this book was not just a restatement of the old, it is a wisdom that took the cultural developments of the day seriously. The author rethought and re-cast his traditions in a new and relevant way, very much like Pope John XXIII did when he called the Second Vatican Council to read the "signs of the times." Like the writer of the Book of Wisdom, the Council Fathers applied the ancient wisdom of the church to a contemporary world and produced the Council documents that guide the church today in living the Catholic Christian life.

My friends, we live in a world of almost unlimited choice, but unfortunately we do not always have the wisdom to make good choices. All day, every day, we are bombarded with "pick me, try me, listen to me, trust me and believe me!" We are free to pick almost anything from these options, but often our freedom includes the freedom to do ourselves in. A host of choices in a climate of freedom is actually dangerous without the wisdom to be able to make good choices. Bad choices, unfortunately, do not just have adverse affects on the person who made the bad choice, but also on everyone around them. We are all victims of people who make bad choices, people with the power to choose, but without the capacity to choose wisely.

My friends, how do you make choices? Are your decisions based on wisdom or on expedience, convenience, popularity and impulsiveness? Can you review all the options available to you, weigh them against a set of guiding principles and then make wise decisions, or are do you just react and grab what feels good, what merely works for you, what meets your needs at the moment? Are you knowledgeable about God's wisdom and the wisdom of God's people in the Scriptures? Do you, like the writer of the Book of Wisdom, review this wisdom, apply it to the reality of your life and make your choices based on this information? If you cannot do this on your own, do you trust the teaching authority of the church to guide you? Only an ignorant and arrogant person would dismiss the wisdom of the ages. Only an ignorant and arrogant person would ignore the power of the wisdom of God's people over centuries to guide one's conduct in speech and deportment, to foster one's own success and advancement and to live free of anxiety which arises from hostility, opposition and failure. It is here we find guidance for living from the collective experience of millions: advice on truthfulness, moderation, chastity, kindliness, honesty and other basic virtues of society. There is a world of difference between trying to reconstruct some bygone world and applying its wisdom to a new world. If we do not learn this lesson soon, we too will watch our culture collapse like all the great cultures of the past. Historians will say about us, "they were a bunch of smart people who did enough dumb things to do themselves in, individually and collectively."

November 10, 1996

A Support System for a
Community of Changing Hearts:
A Parish School of Spiritual
Growth and Education

♥

Announcing The Vision

For the vision still has its time, presses on to fulfillment, and will not disappoint; If it delays, wait for it, it will surely come, it will not be late.

HABAKKUK 2

———— ♥ ————

Today, I want to step out of my regular preaching schedule and give one of the most important talks I have given in this Cathedral. For the last several weeks, I have been involved in a process of deep reflection on the future of our parish and on some of the things I have been hearing from you recently. I have carefully put my reflections into words so that I could present them to you today. I am excited about what I have to say, because it involves proposing a new path for our future. I hope you will give me your undivided attention. I have so much to say and so little time to say it, so let me get right to it.

The Cathedral of the Assumption Parish has changed drastically over the last thirteen years. We have grown from a parish of one hundred ten members, a few visitors, one parish program and an annual budget of $93,000, to a parish of over two thousand members, thousands of visitors, a host of new programs and a budget of almost $800,000, not to mention the resources contributed by the Cathedral

Heritage Foundation. When we first started this experiment, we were certainly not a family-centered parish. We attracted mostly single young adults and Catholics who had been alienated from the church for one reason or another. But gradually over the past thirteen plus years, many of those single young adults got married and had kids. Many of those kids are coming into their teenage years. Likewise, many of those alienated Catholics who returned to the church during those years have settled in, become active and are now the backbone of most parish ministries. Yes, indeed! We have changed.

Our first vision was an ambitious dream of reviving the Cathedral parish. That dream has come true. Our second vision was to expand our programs and renovate our facilities. A large chunk of that dream has been realized as well. Under the leadership of the Cathedral Heritage Foundation, we have created useful new space in the Undercroft, we have been given back a restored old school building. We have renovated the residence, we have purchased property for a garden, we have restored the inside of the church, and we have put up the shell of other new facilities. Even though you see no construction going on right now, preparatory work continues for the next phase of construction. A lot of the money has been and continues to be raised from the community. I believe we will see construction resume in the near future so that the final parts of that dream can come true as well.

It struck me during my weeks of deep reflection, now that those two dreams have been or are almost realized, we need a new dream, a third dream: a dream that addresses our new reality as an established parish with rapidly expanding program needs.

Many of you who have been around for a long time have sensed that things have changed since we came up from the Undercroft to this beautifully renovated worship space, and have said to me, "Things are not like they used to be." Some have even blamed the building. It's not the building. We have changed. We have grown up. In any parish revitalization, the logical second step, after welcoming and incorporating huge numbers of new people, is to make sure we continue to offer on-going spiritual nourishment to those same people as they continue to grow in the faith.

It is in response to these real changes that I want to propose our third vision. Today I want to unveil our new Cathedral Parish School of Catholic Spiritual Growth and Education for adults that will begin this Fall.

During all these years of growth and expansion, I have challenged you over and over again to take responsibility for your own spiritual growth, to be your own spiritual directors. You continue to say to me, "OK, but how?" When you leave here today, you will be offered a booklet that answers that question. This forty-four page booklet outlines a new vision for adult Catholic-Christian formation here at the Cathedral. It will be called "The Cathedral Parish School of Catholic Spiritual Growth and Education."

The church's old model for religious education had many good points, but it had a major weakness. In years past the training in Catholic schools, seminaries and novitiates was carefully arranged so external conformity, at least, could almost be guaranteed by an army of priests, sisters and brothers. One's internal commitment might have been rather weak, but the external supports propping up that commitment were quite powerful. Now that system has collapsed, exposing a weakness in conviction and commitment. There is no one around any more to make us be good. We need to find a new way to help people develop the inner strength to freely choose to live the Catholic faith or else we will continue to unravel as a church despite all our attempts at "renewal". Our lack of spiritual maturity, inner strength, self-discipline and moral courage is destroying our churches, our marriages, our families and neighborhoods. No church, no marriage, no family, no neighborhood, and no country can be strong when everyone in it is weak.

Spiritual maturity cannot be legislated, imposed, bought or borrowed from others. It has to be freely chosen. It has to be developed from within. There is no other way out of our societal messes than to assist massive numbers of people in taking responsibility for developing their own spiritual health, inner strength and moral courage. Without this inner strength, people will not have the ability to keep commitments, to maintain boundaries, to live amidst temptation without giving into it, to make good choices from multiple options, to take responsibility for their actions, to handle freedom without turning it into license, and to have the ability to live from principle rather than convenience. Our school of spirituality seeks to build people from the inside out through helping people develop their own personal spiritual growth plan, to help people freely embrace the challenges of the gospel and to consciously live out of that awareness.

We have created something great here, but we cannot rest on our laurels. Remember, if we are not busy being born, we are busy dying! As we move into our third vision, let's remember the words of St. Francis we used when we started this adventure. "Trust God. Believe in yourself. Dare to Dream."

Excerpt from "A Third Vision," September 8, 1996

190

Outlining The Vision

Every religion has a mystical core. The challenge is to find access to it and live in its power. In this sense, every generation of believers is challenged anew to make its religion truly religious.

BROTHER DAVID STEINDL-RAST, OSB

———— ♥ ————

Perhaps the most interesting trend in contemporary culture is the intense search on the part of Americans for spiritual moorings in life. In that sense, these are the best of times and the worst of times. The old structures of religious institutions and community life are continuing to break down, while at the same time we are well into a new spiritual awakening. As during all previous "great awakenings," there is a shift from religion mediated by authorities to one of direct spiritual experience.

After the Emperor Constantine made Christianity the state religion of the Roman Empire in the fourth century, Christianity as a world religion has sometimes tended to obscure what might be called Christianity as an inner path. Over the years, elements in the Christian tradition which were meant to enable the inner path have often become more important than that inner path itself.

In general, religion takes two forms: the *exoteric* and the *esoteric*. Followers of the *exoteric* approach subscribe to the doctrines, precepts, and rituals of their churches and synagogues, satisfied to relate to the transcendent without experiencing it directly. Followers of the *esoteric* approach, acknowledging that beliefs and rituals only point the way to an experiential goal, journey inward to merge with the transcendent ground of their being. We need both approaches, but unfortunately, churches don't always nourish the transcendental hunger we feel for this living experience of God. Recently, the number of people in the West who are seeking mystical experience has been increasing. Many of them report that their participation in mainstream religious institutions has left a void. These institutions frequently seem unable to guide them to interiority. Sensing that their religious education is incomplete, many people are exploring the Christian mystical writings of people like St. John of the Cross, St. Theresa of Avila, and Meister Eckhart, and rediscovering such traditional spiritual practices as prayer, fasting, meditation and study.

This appetite for spirituality, a religion that transforms, continues to surface more strongly each year at the Cathedral in letters, evaluations and surveys. We have heard more than once, "Yes, I will accept the challenge of taking responsibility for my own spiritual nourishment and growth. Now, how do I do it?"

This hunger for spiritual growth among adults in the Cathedral parish offers us both the opportunity and the challenge to approach adult religious education in our parish in a new way. The goal is to wake us up to God's presence, to nourish that awareness in each of us, and to support each other in living out that awareness of God's presence. We hope to take individual adults through a series of steps within a Catholic parish that will lead to a personal spiritual growth plan. This first part of the program will focus on giving people the basic spiritual tools they will need. The second part of the program will offer these individual Catholics a smorgasbord of spiritual and religious classes and experiences from which they can choose to nourish themselves individually and in small groups on their particular spiritual path. The third part of the program will be made up of advanced courses and even the possibility of teaching others.

Maybe we should include a word about what this is **not**! We are not primarily focused on reforming organizational structures or defending positions in church politics. For some, rage has become a religion. Some believe the church can be fixed with organizational tinkering or with finding a like-minded savior-leader. We believe the fastest and best way to fix the church is by attending to the spiritual health of its members. To paraphrase de Tocqueville, "...a [church] cannot be strong when individuals belonging to it are weak." The great turmoil in religion today is caused by a spirit demanding interiority.

This program is also not about individualistic piety that avoids the world. Our religion is communal. Nothing will change for the better until we have a global revolution of moral consciousness. Our spirituality program will invite adult Catholic Christians to strengthen moral consciousness in a culture that denies the mystical impulses, promotes negative addictions to drugs, crime, and consumerism and violence. Our social problems have at their root a spiritual crisis. Dealing with the spiritual crisis will lead us to cooperate with God's work of healing ourselves as well as the world.

In short, we would like to facilitate excursions to an inner world whose vision then would infuse all parts of the person's life. This is a process that has an entry point, a way to map progress and continues throughout a life-time. The Cathedral Parish School program is designed so that people can enter at different times, and progress in learning at whatever pace each seeker chooses. The program is tailored to suit people from various backgrounds and educational levels. This process is set up to help individuals act on their responsibility for their own spiritual growth by study, reflection, and prayer in the company of other adult Catholics.

In this school, there are no tests, no papers to write, and no tuition. No one graduates. Spiritual growth is a life-long process.

Excerpt from the first course catalogue
for the Cathedral School of Adult Formation and Education
September, 1996

Living The Vision
by Becky Jo Hollingsworth

But how can they call on him in whom they have not
  believed?
And how can they believe in him of whom they have not
  heard?
And how can they hear without someone to preach?
And how can people preach unless they are sent?

ROMANS 10

———— ♥ ————

I number myself among those "disaffected" Christians to whom Father Knott preached so passion-
ately from the Cathedral pulpit. In 1983 I had returned to my hometown to attend graduate school, and by
1987 I had tentatively begun to explore my long-ignored
Christian heritage. I had spent, by then, almost three years
as a hospice social worker and "how can they call on him in
whom they have not believed?" had become a very personal
question. I witnessed the critical difference faith made for
those who are believers as they face death. I had worked
with four very capable chaplains who provided pastoral care
not only to hospice families, but also to their boss. But I
still carried with me a bag full of religious misinformation,
frightening images of a vengeful God and some deeply bur-

ied wounds from my childhood religious formation in a fundamentalist church.

So acute was the conflict between my history and my present experience that I almost never got closer to the Cathedral than the sidewalk outside. Father Knott's commitment to hospitality included standing on the sidewalk outside the massive, peeling doors of the church, greeting worshippers as they arrived. He was usually joined by Father Bill Medley, then associate pastor of the Cathedral parish. My panic about even the most casual interaction set in the first three times I tried to attend Mass at the Cathedral. I spotted Father Knott or Father Medley on the sidewalk, immediately turned around and walked the other way. Finally, on the fourth try in December, 1987, I found the sidewalk blessedly empty. I scurried through the smaller side door, climbed the stairs past a restroom and found myself in the Cathedral at last!

To be perfectly honest, after all that struggle, the place wasn't much to look at once I got inside. Orderly ranks of wooden pews were mostly empty. The stained, frayed carpet which had once been bright gold contrasted badly with stark white walls blotched by peeling paint and stains from old water leaks. The walls were broken by dark, drafty stained glass windows and ugly black pipes ran along the vaulted ceiling. Still, there was a welcoming quiet and a scattering of people who seemed to be intently praying. When the Mass began I was delighted to hear the sonorous chords of an excellent pipe organ and even more pleased that the opening hymn was one with which I was familiar, "O Come, O Come, Emmanuel." The homilist focused on "waiting in patient hope," and the message seemed tailored for me. I listened to the congregation pray the Lord's Prayer (I would later learn to refer to it by its Catholic name — the "Our Father"). Mostly, I wondered when and why I had abandoned saying it myself.

While Father Knott pondered "what to say to a congregation in need of renewal" I pondered questions about my own spiritual life. Having learned to arrive thirty minutes early to avoid sidewalk hospitality, I found myself joining other early Mass arrivals in contemplation and prayer every week, a regular spiritual practice I had neglected for almost twenty years. For the next few months I listened to preaching unlike any in my experience. The preaching in the churches of my childhood and adolescence was certainly intense, but I had never heard such a consistently convincing presentation of God's love for me. Father Knott's homilies, and those of Father Joe Stoltz and the late Father Peyton Badgett, introduced me to a God who bore only the slightest resemblance to the one with whom I thought I was acquainted. In particular, Father Knott's direct, self-revealing stories and explanations encouraged me and gave me hope in a loving God who was almost too good to be true!

I found that I was not alone, and my story not so unique, when I joined a group of six other adults in the Cathedral's RCIA program in the fall of 1988. We ranged in age from early twenties to early sixties and had all been baptized in another Christian tradition, but we shared a common response to the preaching we were hearing Sunday by Sunday. We soon learned that our enthusiasm was shared by some lifelong Catholics and a former Lutheran minister who joined our RCIA group as sponsors and teachers. Together we explored our spiritual hungers and encouraged one another as we prayed together. We found we all had stories of discouragement and we all struggled with issues of faith

197

and doctrine. We unearthed nuggets of good from what for many of us had been a rubble of religious formation, like my discovery that the intense exposure to Scripture study in my Baptist childhood gave me a familiarity and comfort with the Bible for which some cradle Catholics long.

Soon after my reception into the Church at the Easter Vigil in 1989, the leadership of the parish chose to invest more parish resources in the area of formation and hired the Cathedral's first full-time director of religious education, Patricia A. Sexton. Mrs. Sexton's previous experience in other parishes and her wise leadership were welcome additions to a parish staff which had already witnessed a tripling in the number of parishioners, almost all of them adults, in the preceding six years. The parish had recently completed the three year RENEW program but no organized program of formation for adult Catholics had followed it, leaving RCIA and a small Bible study group as the only ongoing adult formation programs in the parish.

At this, almost the midpoint of Father Knott's tenure as pastor of the Cathedral, the greatest period of growth and change for the Cathedral parish still lay ahead. By the time the Cathedral Parish School of Catholic Spiritual Growth and Education enrolled its first class of spiritual seekers in September, 1995, the parish community would number almost two thousand households. In this chapter, I hope to give the reader some insight into the "view from the pews" to complement the words from the pulpit which compose most of this book. In my words, and the words of some of the more than two hundred adults who have enrolled in the Cathedral School courses, I hope to encourage other spiritual teachers and seekers to persevere in "asking, seeking and knocking." I hope to do this through sharing some of the stories of adult, conscious Catholic Christians who have committed between three to eight hours per week to serious study of their spiritual life and Catholic faith.

One of my favorite ways to renew my spirit is by gardening, and I think of the period between 1989 and 1995 as the period during which an initially small, but steadily increasing number of lay people stepped forward to help nurture the seedlings of renewed spiritual life which were sprouting in changed hearts. By 1989 a core group of lay leaders had broken ground by organizing an Education Committee and they collaborated with the pastoral staff in taking to heart St. Paul's challenge to a small but rapidly growing congregation in Rome — "And how can people preach unless they are sent?" This core group of gardeners was soon joined by others who embraced the challenge they were hearing from the pulpit to shoulder their responsibility for their own spiritual vitality and that of their community.

Many lifelong Catholics did this first by volunteering as sponsors or catechists in RCIA, extending support and spiritual companionship to new believers and baptized Christians like me who were resuming a serious commitment to their spiritual lives within the Roman Catholic Church. A number of those lifelong Catholics confessed in planning meetings and RCIA sessions that their investment in mentoring us new Catholics was strongly motivated by a desire to learn more about their own Catholic faith and heritage. Those of us involved in recruiting volunteers to meet the need for RCIA sponsors were confronted fairly often with the need to reassure lifelong Catholics that they did not have to know all the answers in Scripture or in catechism to exercise a ministry as sponsors. We were confronted, too, with many adult Catholics who wished to join the RCIA groups not as sponsors or catechists or hospitality ministers, but as participants — as spiritual seekers exploring their Catholic Christianity for the first time as adults. As more than one member of my parish community said to me, "I'm not sure I would be a good sponsor. I haven't really had any religious education since I got out of high school. But can I come to the RCIA sessions anyway?"

We learned from inviting some of these adult Catholics to participate in the RCIA program that, while this worked for a few, neither the formation needs of the spiritually hungry adults who were already fully initiated Catholics nor the formation needs of those seeking to join a Catholic parish for the first time were meet well by combining them in one program. The needs expressed by these two groups were similar in the essentials. Both groups consistently expressed the desire to learn more about the message and life of Jesus, about the Scriptures and the traditions of the Church which have evolved to preserve this message through almost two thousand years of human history, and about the wisdom of those faithful disciples who believe the ever-powerful good news of God's love for each one of us. But the "viewing point" from which members of both groups approached these shared needs for formation in the Christian life often gave rise to frustration for all of us. It became apparent that addressing the questions raised by adult Catholics about their spiritual renewal **within** their "native" tradition often took time away from the serious questions of those approaching from **outside** that tradition, and vice versa. As more and more people in both groups flocked to the Cathedral, attracted by the excellent liturgy and preaching, it became apparent that we needed to break even more new ground in which the renewed faith of a large number of recommitted spiritual seekers could take root and grow.

Under the leadership of Mrs. Sexton and Father Knott, a core group of four lay parishioners were called upon to serve as the Adult Formation Committee for the Cathedral parish. We were challenged to imagine and explore new ways to meet the demand for information, guidance and instruction in the spiritual life from adults in the parish. Between 1992 and 1995, we tried out a variety of approaches — everything from weekly book study groups to monthly lectures on issues in contemporary Roman Catholic thought and practice. We organized and presented seasonal days of reflection and group discussions in which parishioners reflected on some of Father Knott's homilies which form the second section of this volume. We planned some offerings that lasted two hours, some that lasted two hours a week for a few weeks, and some that lasted two hours a week for twenty-six weeks for two years. We sought the counsel of staff members of the archdiocesan Office of Lifelong Formation and attended meetings with people from other parishes to learn from each other. We held focus groups attended by more than seventy-five adults who provided us with invaluable feedback about what topics interested them and how much time they were willing to commit to their own spiritual nourishment. We concentrated on utilizing sound principles of adult learning with participants, aware that for many their last religious education experiences had been in childhood or adolescence. Not every program we planned bore lots of fruit. Some were frankly failures, like one small group I led, at the end of which four hardy participants gave me an honest assessment about how their expectations had been disappointed. Most, though, attracted enough enthusiastic participants to convince us that a community of serious spiritual seekers had indeed formed at the Cathedral. Moreover, this group of early participants began to form a nucleus of volunteers willing to take on assignments to promote, host, administer, teach and provide hospitality for future offerings.

By the early autumn of 1994 the Adult Formation Committee had planned what seemed to us to be an ambitious program of adult formation offerings for the coming year, the year in which we as a parish would see a dream come true. Renovation of the interior of the Cathedral was almost completed. On Thanksgiving Day the parish community would celebrate its first liturgy together in the transformed interior of the Cathedral church, following celebrations with the whole archdiocese and the larger Louisville community which had so generously supported the restoration of our historic buildings. After a lengthy period of construction that touched every one of us in one way or another, (it usually got me in the sinuses — it really was a dust bowl!) we were a parish ready and eager to celebrate the end of an exile from our worship space which had lasted twice as long as originally planned. In particular, those of us involved in formation ministries looked forward to having more space for religious education classes and formation offerings for both the children and adults of a parish whose membership continued to both grow and grow up.

It was about this time that Father Knott began to talk with those of us in parish leadership positions about a "new vision" for the parish community which would support the continued renewal of the parish far past the rehabilitation of its physical plant. In homilies and in conversations, he reflected with many of us that the immense gifts and efforts required to plan, finance and do the work of restoring the Cathedral's buildings required more than merely even our most sincere appreciation of the gifts God had bestowed on us as a parish. These efforts, impressive as they were, were basically the response of grateful hearts to the news of God's faithfulness and love for us — one heart at a time. The beauty and light of the restored church interior might continue to attract those who needed to hear some good news and see some beauty, but it would be the hospitality and prayerfulness of those of us within that building week in and week out which determined whether the hundreds of visitors, guests and spiritual seekers would feel the presence of God. It was up to us to take responsibility for using well the many blessings we had been given. It was up to us, as maturing Catholic Christians, to nurture each other as we continued our spiritual growth. It was up to us to see that a beautifully restored Cathedral did not become "a dusty monument" within our lifetimes and those of our children, but remained a center of spiritual growth and energy.

In late 1994, Father Knott attended a meeting of the Adult Formation Committee and sketched out his ideas for how this ongoing renewal might be nourished. As he mentions in several of the homilies in this book, he was hearing over and over from parishioners who were ready to take up the challenge but felt ill-prepared for being sent forth to "preach to those who had not heard." Father Knott told the committee that his reflections on what to say to those who responded to the challenge by asking, "OK, how do we do it?" had given him the idea for a "Cathedral School of Spirituality," a planned series of classes for adults that would span three years. Students in the school would be expected to make a significant commitment of time to learning about the "inner path" in an organized series of classes which would both teach skills for the spiritual life and impart information about our Catholic faith and tradition. As individuals completed self-designed programs of spiritual growth, they could in turn be expected to share their faith with those to whom they had been sent in "preach" in families, workplaces, civic and social groups and within the parish walls.

For my fellow committee members and me, these ideas about how to organize the resources and energy we were already devoting to adult formation served as a catalyst for bringing together a coherent program through which the needs of very different adults could be met. The idea of a "school" gave us a framework within which to distill the experiences and feedback of the preceding few years. Throughout the early part of 1995 we held long meetings during which we planned a core curriculum and tried to envision how such a School would operate. We looked back over what we had learned over the years from the people we hoped would be the School's first students. We designed an orientation session which would be mandatory for all new students and settled on a series of twelve courses on Scripture, church history, Catholic theology and the spiritual disciplines. Our planning sessions were lively, even heated sometimes as we struggled to flesh out a new model of adult formation in the parish.

It soon became apparent that more resources would be needed to carry off this ambitious program. In early 1996 the parish leadership and parish pastoral staff made commitments to include funding for a part-time teacher for the Cathedral School in the budget for the upcoming year. Father Knott is fond of quoting the saying that "When the student is ready, the teacher will appear." And so it was for us. Dr. Marylee King, SCN, preparing to retire after a distinguished tenure at Spalding University where she taught Scripture and theology courses, was looking for an opportunity to continue the teaching she loved, but "without tests, grades or committee meetings," as she would later tell me. She joined the parish staff in July, 1996 and immediately set about planning the first two courses on "The Spiritual Disciplines" and "Introduction to Scripture: Jesus, the Human Face of God." Meanwhile, those of us on the Adult Formation Committee concentrated on "getting the word out." In this, we were ably assisted by Bobie Jo Bilz, Father Knott's secretary, who took on the myriad tasks involved in the layout and publication of a forty-four page catalogue which would be distributed to every parish household, and who endured and deciphered the drafts of four different writers with patience and good grace.

About a week before the "grand opening," the five of us on the Adult Formation Committee gathered for one final meeting. We reviewed and fine-tuned plans for hospitality, registration, audio and video taping of the orientation sessions. We did the same for the first two class sessions which would be held the following week. We were anxious to create a comfortable environment and a smooth operation to welcome a still unknown number of students. We swapped stories of the enthusiastic responses we had heard from people who had read the catalogue. In the midst of discussions about coffeepots and keys, we got to the question of how many copies we should make of the handouts for the orientation sessions. I said I thought thirty-five would be an excellent turnout. Pat Sexton, always more optimistic and usually more accurate than me, suggested we make enough for fifty.

Less than one hour in to the first orientation session we had made not one, but two trips back to the copy machine to make additional handouts for the more than one hundred-fifty spiritual seekers who streamed into the

Undercroft that night. In the two and a half years since that night more than two hundred adults have attended one or more classes in the Cathedral School. These students have devoted an average of five hours per week to class attendance and study. A sizeable minority of these students have taken every class offered. Some adults who have not attended a class have borrowed the audio or video tapes made of every class to use for personal study.

In preparing to write this chapter I was blessed by the opportunity to listen to the answers to these questions:

- Looking back at the classes you've taken, which were most important or significant for you? What made these classes stand out?
- What topics or areas do you wish had been presented in this first three years?
- Tell us something about how your experience in the Cathedral School has changed, strengthened or hampered your spiritual life.
- What experiences or topics should we be sure to offer in the near future?

I posed these questions to more than one hundred of my fellow parishioners who were enrolled in "Praying With the Psalms," one of the Cathedral School courses offered in November, 1998. Over fifty adults took time to share their reflections on these and other questions with me in person and in writing, individually and in small groups. Both Pat Sexton and Sister Marylee King embraced the idea of seeking answers to these questions with enthusiasm, and their personal reflections have been of immense help to me in making sense (I hope) out of the feedback we gathered. Most of all, I am grateful to the people who agreed to share the stories of their spiritual lives with me. From their stories of patience, endurance, searching and grace I reaped a rich personal harvest of inspiration and yet more proof that this process of renewal works.

What follows is a sample of what these people had to say in answer to the questions above. There was a high degree of agreement among the answers to the first question. Almost all of those who had taken classes in the first two years reported that the courses on Scripture and the course on prayer had made the most impact on their lives. The introductory course on the gospels drew praise from one student who reported that she had "never read any of the gospels. It's been a revelation to me! For me it was the perfect preparation for the class on prayer." Another humble student put it this way: "It is very difficult to choose any good, better or best, but since I have always had problems making much sense from the books of the Old Testament I must choose those classes as the most meaningful to me. (I think I have graduated from nursery school and am ready for kindergarten.) . . . Since attending I have found the Sunday readings far more meaningful. . . . In summation, the classes have given me the realization and perspective that the Bible is a living document, not just a dusty old tome." One student spoke of a growth in self-confidence when talking with other adults at work and in social situations which she attributes to the Scripture classes: "It's given me confidence because others can read and quote the Bible better than Catholics can." Two students, a married couple, reported that their commitment to preparing for the prayer course together had lead to the first serious discussions of their spiritual lives with each other since they had completed the preparations for their marriage twenty years before. "We both knew that the church was important to us and seldom missed Mass. We just never talked about it. We didn't pray together either, beyond grace at meals with the family. We started dropping in to the Cathedral a few years ago whenever we're downtown and we happened to be there the Sunday Father Ron preached about the new classes that were starting. We were at a low point as a couple, and we had just started talking about setting aside time for a 'date' each week. After reading the catalogue, we decided that we would meet downtown for dinner on Wednesday nights, then go to the class together. I had no idea I was about to fall in love with my wife, and with God, all over again."

The concurrence of opinion among my respondents also held for the second question, which solicited their feedback about what had been lacking in the curriculum during the first two years. "Don't change a thing!" was the response I heard most frequently. A few students did offer thoughtful criticism of some content and some of the ways individual courses had been structured. Students likewise had a few suggestions for courses to be taught in the near future (question four) but the majority agreed that they were ready for more advanced courses on prayer and Scripture. Many mentioned looking forward to the class on church history scheduled for January, 1999.

Throughout the discussions of curriculum, past and future, what was most evident was the respect and esteem in which students held Sister Marylee. This was particularly evident to me when I gathered with Sister Marylee, Pat Sexton and seventeen students for a group discussion in late November, 1998. In the interactions between students and teacher, both before and during the discussion, it was patent that a mutual love affair was going on. One student gave voice to the sentiments of many others: "I'll sign-up for any class you decide to teach." Sister Marylee, in turn, paid tribute to the dedication of her students, saying that she had been inspired and challenged by the serious commitment to their own spiritual growth the students had shown. Many students also expressed their appreciation for Pat Sexton's leadership and for the guidance and support she had offered many of them individually. About half my respondents mentioned feeling grateful to the parish for supporting the Cathedral School. One student told me: "I move around a lot with my job, and I counted up one day that I had been a member of eight parishes. Nowhere else have I ever seen anything like these classes. I don't think I've ever even heard all that much about the need for adults to keeping learning about their spiritual life. I wish I could round up a few former pastors and drag them along to these classes. I think they would be surprised at what's going on here."

The responses to the third question — an invitation to speak to how the students' spiritual lives had been helped or hindered by participation in the School — produced stories as individual as the people themselves. Many students told me about a deepening prayer life which had, in the words of one student, "given me a personal God." Another person spoke with passion and enthusiasm about the blessings she attributed to learning to create "a conversational space with God." One young single mother laughed as she recalled her struggle to teach her two elementary school-aged children to respect "Mom's Meditation Time," short periods that she introduced into the family routine to carve out enough time to read the text for upcoming classes or write in the spiritual journal she had begun to keep. "I knew that something had really **changed** in our family one day last month. We had all had 'one of those days.' The kids were cranky and I was on my last nerve because of stuff at work. A squabble broke out between the kids about something, and I played referee for what seemed like the hundredth time that morning. Finally, in exasperation, I decided to declare an unscheduled Mom's Meditation Time and firmly shut the door to my bedroom, telling the kids 'I just need fifteen minutes of peace and quiet.' When I opened the door at the end of that quarter hour, I was startled to see my son and daughter sitting quietly right outside the door. I asked them if everything was OK and my oldest piped up with: 'Well, Mom's Meditation Time always seems to make you feel better. We decided we could **really** use some Kid's Meditation Time this morning!"

Almost half of the students I interviewed were volunteers in one of the Cathedral parish's many ministries. I asked some of these respondents to describe the impact of what they had learned on their lay ministry. This proved to be a somewhat difficult question for many to answer. As one man put it, "I don't think I do all that much differently. I know I **am** more aware of why I volunteer and who I'm trying to serve. I do pray more often before I start, but whether anyone else can see a difference I really don't know." One student who volunteers in the Ministry to the Homebound, said this: "I did find that the Scripture classes made me more comfortable reading and talking about the Sunday readings. I started offering to read the Sunday readings to the folks I visit and then told them a little about the homily." Many respondents spoke to the impact of their studies on that most fundamental of the lay ministries, being "full, conscious and active" participants in liturgy, agreeing that they listened more intently during the Liturgy of the Word and experienced a deeper, more intense prayer during the Liturgy of the Eucharist. Some also articulated the difference their study had made in their work-related roles. One student, a teacher, related that she had adopted the practice of praying alone in her classroom at the beginning and end of each school day. "I've always said a prayer for the children in my class at Mass, but this daily prayer has definitely made me a better teacher — more patient — and I think I work harder to see the gifts in every child." One student reported seeking a new job as her personal prayer experiences lead her to become increasingly uncomfortable with the business practices of a former employer. Another student, a small business owner, reported that he found himself trying to consider the needs of his employees more carefully in his business decisions, a change he attributed directly to his increased study of the gospels.

A few students talked about feeling lost during the first few weeks of class and for some this evoked some anger. A student spoke of her determination to hang in there even though "I didn't understand half of what Sister Marylee was talking about. I got mad thinking about how different some things in my life might have been if I'd learned the basics when I was younger. But I'm a post-Vatican II Catholic. We sat around in high school religion classes and talked about butterflies." This student had company among her class-mates, another of whom commented: "I never studied so hard in my life. It helped that Sister Marylee kept reassuring me that it would get clearer. And it did." One woman sounded more wistful than angry when she spoke of the excitement she felt about what she was learning: "One of my children joined the local 'mega-church' a few years ago. Maybe if his religious education had been this exciting he would have stayed a Catholic."

Other students spoke of instances when something they heard in class unlocked the floodgates of memory about

211

being scared, shamed, demeaned or bored in religious education earlier in their lives. They spoke of individual struggles to "learn to view the church with adult compassion," and about the many ways they reached out for help in their struggles, some for the first time in their lives. At least ten students reported seeking the Sacrament of Reconciliation as part of this growth, one man after an absence of almost twenty-five years. A few individuals had sought out spiritual directors; some of these were disappointed in how difficult it was to find one as they contacted potential directors who had no open time in their schedules. Many class members turned to one another for support in these matters, in a creative medley of small study groups, one-on-one relationships of spiritual companionship that included regular meetings for prayer and study, or larger groups that had begun sharing meals and discussion about class materials. One student summarized the impact of the classes on her in this way: "Your question made me think. I really enjoy going to the classes, but I have to ask myself, do you really change? I think the answer is yes — but it takes awhile."

One of the most poignant and moving stories came from one of the School's newest students and I want to quote her at length. The student had taken only two classes, those offered in Fall, 1998. Her comments begin with a tribute to another student, whose "preaching" lead to a life-changing experience for her.

Several weeks ago my friend and boss [a Cathedral parishioner] told me I should consider attending the Cathedral class devoted to the Book of Revelation. [She] has some knowledge of my family history and how the early 'religious' teaching I received from them had affected me. I was intrigued when she said, . . . 'Everything you've been taught is wrong!'

My mother's family always seemed to be preparing to celebrate the Second Coming as though it were going to be the next major holiday. I found this strange, because they also talked about the Second Coming as being preceded by terrible agony and despair for Christians. They were certain that we were on the brink of the Last Days and that surely they would arrive on or before the year 2000. Their 'proof,' as they called it, was the Book of Revelation.

. . . It was difficult for me to reconcile my longing to establish a relationship with a loving God with this expectation of pain and suffering on behalf of this same God. As a result, I slid into denial. I simply stopped thinking about it, which, of course, meant not thinking about God.

So imagine my shock when I heard Sister Marylee King talk about the Book of Revelation as a testimony to God's faithfulness and love. This is NOT a vindictive, sadistic God after all! Imagine my delight during the 'Praying the Psalms' class when I listened to Sister King talk about developing a personal, loving, <u>real</u> relationship with God right now, rather than living in dread of the eventual meeting on Judgement Day.

Long story short. As a result of my participation in the Cathedral's Spiritual Growth classes, I have returned to a relationship with God based on joy and not on fear. I couldn't be happier or more excited! I look forward to enjoying future classes, as I look forward to a deepening relationship with a living, joyful God."

Serious seekers demand solid spiritual nourishment.

213

It seems clear that the adult students who have experienced this new approach to adult formation within the parish have found it. Those of us involved in planning for the near future of the Cathedral School face challenges as we consider how to add more advanced courses while we maintain the entry level courses. We must continue to "get the word out" to those who are ready to mature spiritually. As potential students hear the good news of salvation preached week in and week out from the Cathedral's pulpit, now entrusted to the capable hands of Father Martin Linebach, parochial vicar and Father William Fichteman, our pastor, and as they interact with some of the hundreds of students who are now better equipped to "be sent forth to preach," we as a parish community will continue to be renewed. As we seek to be good stewards of the gifts we have been given, we will be challenged to continue to pay attention to the details and to have the courage to be excellent.

Father Knott opened this book by saying:

> How does one revive a dying parish? It's simple. All you have to do is lead the ones who will spearhead the revitalization to consciously commit to their own serious spiritual transformation, then encourage them to talk about it with passion, regularity, clarity and conviction. Since people are already spiritually starving and looking for spiritual energy, they will hear about it. Little by little, those people who are ready for spiritual transformation will find these teachers. When enough of these seekers and teachers gather together and begin to intersect and interact, they will wake up one day and realize that the parish has been revitalized!

In the margin notes I made on the first draft of his essay I wrote: "It may be simple, but it's sure not easy!" A

Parish School of Spiritual Growth not only takes a vision, it takes a serious collaborative effort between lay parish leaders and the pastoral staff. It takes resources. It takes a lot of work to break new ground, then to sow, water, weed and fertilize the ground for the fruits of the Spirit to emerge. But, as I hope you could hear in the voices of the spiritual seekers I have quoted, a rich harvest will result.

Readers who are not a part of the Cathedral parish community may be tempted to doubt that such a renewal could happen in **their** parishes because they don't have all the resources of a cathedral church. But every Catholic parish has a pulpit. Every Catholic parish has a few lay leaders who could step forward to commit themselves first to their own spiritual growth, and then to that of their parish. And there are more than enough hungry hearts who need to hear about our faithful, loving God, and then be challenged to undertake the process of personal transformation within a community of changed hearts.

January 4, 1999

One Heart At A Time is available from

Inspirations Gift Shop
Cathedral Heritage Foundation
429 W. Muhammad Ali Boulevard, Suite 100
Louisville, Kentucky 40202
(502) 583-3100

———— ♥ ————

Proceeds from the sale of this book will benefit the
Cathedral Heritage Foundation.